CHOOSING THE RIGHT HEALTH CARE PLAN

Choosing the Right Health Care Plan

Henry S. Berman, M.D.,
and Louisa Rose

Consumers Union
Mount Vernon, New York

Library of Congress Cataloging-in-Publication Data
Berman, Henry.
Choosing the right health care plan / Henry S. Berman and Louisa Rose.
p. cm.
Includes bibliographical references.
ISBN 0-89043-218-X (pbk.)
1. Insurance, Health—United States—Handbooks, manuals, etc.
I. Rose, Louisa. II. Title.
HG9396.B48 1990
368.3′82—dc20 88-71029
CIP

Design by Susan Hood

First printing, October 1990
Manufactured in the United States of America

Choosing the Right Health Care Plan is a Consumer Reports Book published by Consumers Union, the nonprofit organization that publishes *Consumer Reports*, the monthly magazine of test reports, product Ratings, and buying guidance. Established in 1936, Consumers Union is chartered under the Not-For-Profit Corporation Law of the State of New York.

The purposes of Consumers Union, as stated in its charter, are to provide consumers with information and counsel on consumer goods and services, to give information on all matters relating to the expenditure of the family income, and to initiate and to cooperate with individual and group efforts seeking to create and maintain decent living standards.

Consumers Union derives its income solely from the sale of *Consumer Reports* and other publications. In addition, expenses of occasional public service efforts may be met, in part, by nonrestrictive, noncommercial contributions, grants, and fees. Consumers Union accepts no advertising or product samples and is not beholden in any way to any commercial interest. Its Ratings and reports are solely for the use of the readers of its publications. Neither the Ratings nor the reports nor any Consumers Union publications, including this book, may be used in advertising or for any commercial purpose. Consumers Union will take all steps open to it to prevent such uses of its materials, its name, or the name of *Consumer Reports*.

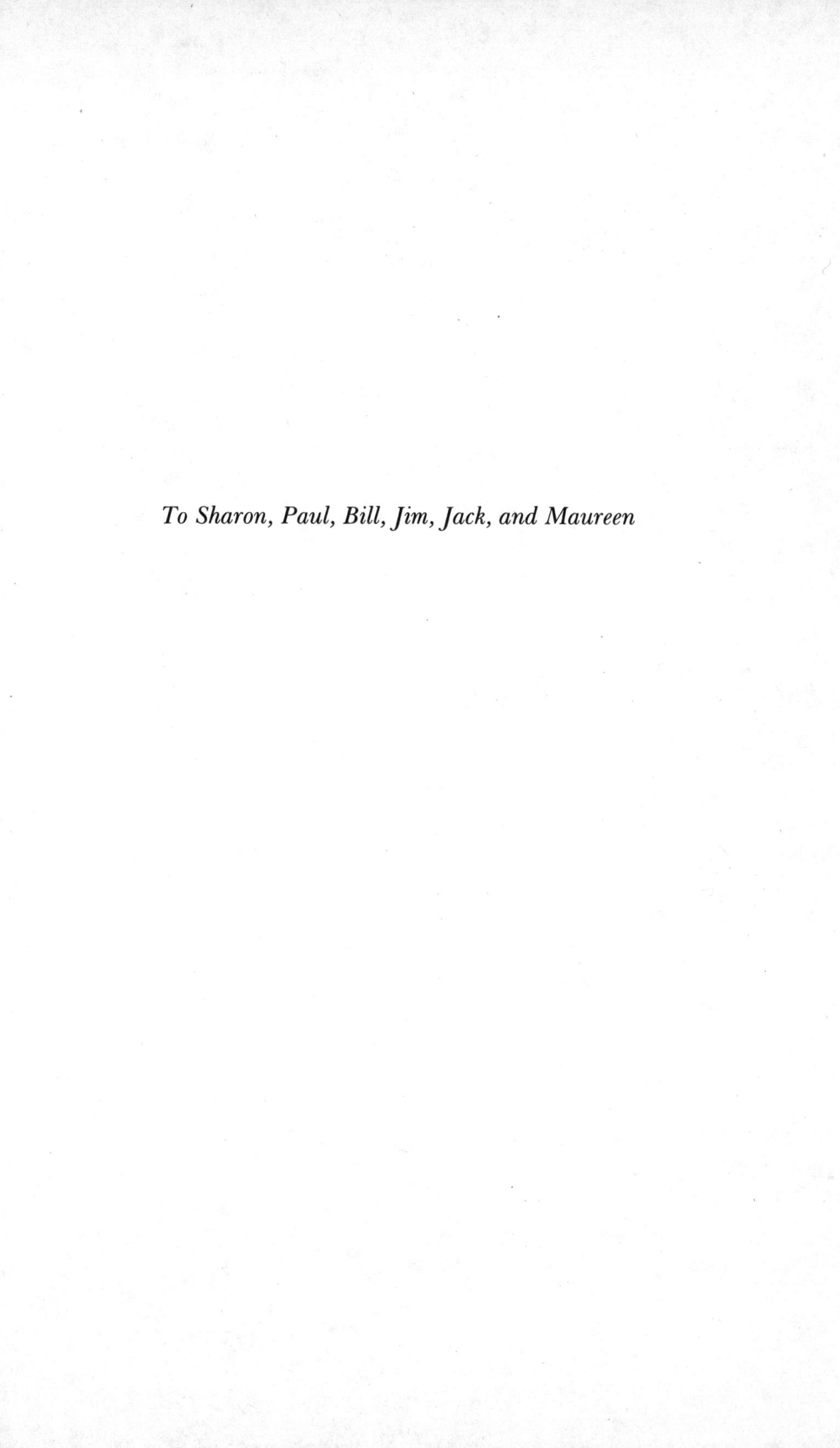

To Sharon, Paul, Bill, Jim, Jack, and Maureen

Contents

Acknowledgments

In the process of writing this book, we received the advice and cooperation of a number of people. In addition to the many health care consumers who were willing to share their experiences and feelings with us, the following experts were particularly helpful in reviewing parts of the manuscript or sharing their expertise: Drs. Leonard Katz, Paul Lenz, Edward Marine, Dennis O'Leary, and Michael Soper; and John Baackes, Christy Bell, Roger Birnbaum, Sharon Fairchild, George Halvorson, Marcus Merz, John Nelson, Barbara Mohr Umbdenstock, M.S.N., Janet Wetmore, and several consultants from The Wyatt Company.

Special thanks to Shelly Carter for all her help, to Seth Schapiro for his good sense and reassurance, and to our agents, Jane Gelfman and Deborah Schneider, for their unwavering support.

INTRODUCTION

Why Health Insurance Will Never Be the Same

In 1980, if you were like 90 percent of the people covered by employer-sponsored health insurance, you didn't give much thought to the type of insurance you had. You simply signed up with the "company plan." Your employer paid the whole premium, or most of it, and you had to satisfy only a fairly small deductible, perhaps $50 or $100, before your insurance kicked in.

When you needed medical care, you did not have to meet any particular conditions before your care was covered. After you had been treated by the doctor or had returned from the hospital, you submitted a claim, and the insurance company reimbursed you for doctors' fees and reimbursed the hospital directly. You enjoyed a virtually unlimited choice of doctors and hospitals, and there was essentially no interference with the decisions you or your physician made.

But times are changing. A survey of businesses conducted in 1987 found that this picture had shifted dramatically: In that year, only 40 percent of employed people had coverage that still allowed such a degree of free choice with virtually no interference. By the early 1990s, it is estimated, only 5 to 10 percent of employees will have such coverage.[1] The rest will enroll in plans that, in various ways, "manage" their care.

And those people who must buy their own individual policies are finding fewer health insurance plans that they can afford or that will accept them; individual plans that offer the kinds of freedom of choice that were common a decade ago are rare indeed.

When you go shopping for health insurance nowadays, you will discover that you must make trade-offs among a confusing array of plans. Some employers offer ten or more different health insurance plans, each with its own set of rules, benefits, and limitations, and each specifying different combinations of physicians and hospitals. At one extreme you will find "cost-managing" plans that give you unlimited freedom to select your own physicians and hospitals. These plans, however, impose certain limits on other kinds of choice. They may require prior approval by the insurance company for elective hospital admissions and surgical procedures, mandate that certain procedures be performed in an outpatient setting, and oblige you to seek a second opinion (a formal process discussed in detail on page 4) before you have elective surgery.

At the other end of the spectrum you will find "managed care" plans, such as group practice Health Maintenance Organizations (HMOs). These organizations require you to receive all your medical care from HMO physicians practicing in the HMO's health care centers. If you need hospital care, you must be admitted by an HMO doctor to a hospital approved by the HMO, unless you need emergency treatment.

Between these extremes, you will find a number of different kinds of coverage with names drawn from a bowl of alphabet soup. There are CMPs, PPOs, PPAs, EPOs, IPAs—and who knows what other acronyms are about to be born. The good news is that in almost all cases, you get to dip your own spoon into the soup and come up with the plan that seems right for you. The bad news is that not only are the terms confusing, but so are the plans themselves. Furthermore, since the plans are competing with one another for your business, each markets itself in the best possible light, minimizing its limitations or disadvantages. To choose a plan intelligently in today's health insurance market, you must do your own detailed research.

This situation is due primarily to the rising cost of health care. Medical schools have produced a physician surplus, and many of these extra physicians have become high-priced specialists and superspecialists. Hospitals employ a more costly work force as their employees effectively bargain for better pay. Scientists have developed expensive new diagnostic and treatment technology, such as magnetic resonance imaging (a radiological technique to study the inside of the body) and lithotripsy (a nonsurgical treatment for kidney stones and gallstones that uses shock waves). Patients have become more litigious, and the high cost of malpractice insurance is then passed along in the form of higher physicians' fees. Driving costs ever higher is the fact that our population is aging—and older people have more expensive medical problems.

Right now, employers are worried. They have watched health care costs climb from 4.3 percent of the gross national product in the mid-1950s to almost 12 percent by the end of the 1980s. A survey of Fortune 500 chief executive officers conducted jointly by *Fortune* and Cable News Network revealed that only 8 percent of those polled believed that they had been "highly successful" in curbing "wasteful or excessive use of health services"; most judged they had been "moderately successful." One-fifth of these predominantly conservative business leaders stated that they had an increased interest in "some sort of universal national health insurance plan."[2]

Reducing Costs: Employer Initiatives

As health care costs continue to rise, employers, both private and public, are attempting to stem the tide by passing on more of these costs to their employees and by encouraging competition among companies that sell health care insurance.

To help you understand these new plans, we have characterized the ways employers go about cutting costs as "cost-managing," "cost-shifting," and "care-managing." They have been doing all three, and we can expect to see them redouble their efforts along these lines through the 1990s.

Cost-Managing

This is a popular strategy, and it includes some roadblocks for the patient, such as mandatory second opinions before any surgery is performed, preadmission certification, and an emphasis on ambulatory surgery whenever possible.

Second surgical opinions. Employers sat up and took notice when a number of studies appeared showing that the same surgical procedure might be performed twice as often in one part of a state as in another, with no medical reason to explain the variation. Patients in one county were not sicker or genetically different. The variation, it became clear, had something to do with the behavior and beliefs of clusters of physicians. In addition, a number of studies demonstrated that when patients who were told they ought to have surgery talked to a second surgeon, many decided they didn't need it.[3]

Employers who are managing costs usually require, or recommend, that their employees get a second opinion for certain elective procedures. In most cases the employee is free to accept either opinion if the two differ; some employers require that the employee obtain a third opinion if the first two disagree.

Preadmission certification. Because hospital care is the single most expensive element of health care, some employers offer insurance plans that require prior approval for any elective admission. You might have to follow a number of rules about which hospital you can use, whether you must have tests before you are admitted, or how long a stay will be covered if there are no complications. For instance, some plans will cover only a percentage of your hospital bill (50 to 80 percent) if you do not receive authorization prior to admission for elective surgery.

Ambulatory surgery. A decade ago, almost all patients who needed surgery spent at least three days in the hospital, no matter how minor the procedure. Now, many of the simpler surgical procedures are done on an outpatient basis, either in a day-surgery wing of a hospital, at a freestanding ambulatory surgery center, or in a surgical suite located in a physician's office. Employers who use "cost-managing" offer policies that define an extensive list of procedures that must be performed on an ambulatory basis. Such policies may provide no coverage for these procedures if they are performed in a hospital, or reimburse you at a reduced rate—for example, 50 percent coverage instead of 80 percent.

Employers may use a number of other approaches to manage costs. They may send an expert to do "case management" for employees who are hospitalized with serious and expensive illnesses. The expert will evaluate whether using a different treatment plan or another institution could provide effective care to the patient at less cost.

Employers may also hire "claims management" experts to review expensive hospital and physician claims in order to determine whether those claims are appropriate. Some employers even reward employees who find discrepancies in their hospital bills.

Cost-Shifting

Reasoning that costs cannot be reduced unless the health care consumer has a motivation to look for cost-effective care, employers have adjusted the benefits structures of the health insurance plans they offer. Some employers like to call these adjustments "cost-saving," but since they save money for the employer at the expense of their employees, "cost-shifting" is a more accurate term.

Among the most common cost-shifting measures employers use are the following:

Increasing the deductible. The "deductible" is an amount patients must pay before any coverage is available from their insurance. A decade ago, $50 was the most common deductible; now, $200 or more is becoming a standard amount for a single person, while the deductible for a family may be $500 or higher. Employers find that this strategy lowers their expense even beyond the dollar value of the deductible because higher initial costs discourage their employees from seeking care. An unfortunate consequence of high deductibles is that they may cause people to forgo a necessary visit to the doctor.

Raising the co-insurance percentage. The term "co-insurance" refers to a sharing of costs between the insured person and the insurance company according to a defined ratio. In the past, some policies covered 100 percent of medical costs after the deductible was met, and until recently, one-third of large companies such as General Motors and AT&T provided this kind of coverage to their employees. In 1988, General Motors began to require their employees to pay co-insurance, and other employers have been increasing the percentage they require their employees to pay. The 80/20 split that has prevailed for several years is quickly being replaced by a 70/30 split as medical care gets more expensive. Whether the employee is carrying a 20 percent or a 30 percent share, the dollar amount in question is an increasingly significant sum.

Hiking the employees' share of the premium. Another way employers shift costs is to have their employees pay part of the health insurance premium. Many employers who used to pay 100 percent of the premium are now asking employees to pay a share, and those who never covered premiums in full are increasing the amount employees must contribute. For years, federal workers have had a wide choice of plans; now, those who want to continue in plans with extensive benefits and an unrestricted choice of physicians and hospitals must pay hundreds of dollars more *per month* in premiums than do co-workers who choose less comprehensive plans or managed care.

Care-Managing

The third basic strategy in controlling costs is called "care-managing." Employers offer financial incentives to employees to join managed health care plans. These plans use medical resources more economically than other types of plans and negotiate discounts from health care providers and institutions. Health Maintenance Organizations (HMOs) and Preferred Provider Organizations (PPOS) are two types of organized health care systems that attempt to manage care; both restrict their subscribers' choice of physicians or hospitals.

Health Maintenance Organizations (HMOs)

HMOs are prepaid plans that sell insurance coverage and also provide health care, either by hiring physicians or by contracting with them. The insurance coverage they provide is very extensive and plan members have few out-of-pocket expenses. The 1987 survey of businesses discussed earlier found that 16 percent of employees were enrolled in HMOs, and that figure is expected to double by the early 1990s. By offering their employees the option to join HMOs, employers can provide richer benefits and fuller coverage for comparable premiums while holding or even reducing their own costs. Members of HMOs are required to receive all of their care from the physicians and hospitals that the plan designates.

Group practice HMOs. This type of HMO integrates insurance and health care providers into a single operation. Members receive care from physicians who work in health care centers run by the HMO and are covered only for the care authorized by these physicians. Because they are the most tightly managed systems, group practice HMOs generally have the lowest overall costs of any type of managed health care.

Independent Practice Association HMOs (IPAs). The insurance coverage provided by IPA-model HMOs is identical to that offered by group practice HMOs, and your care must be authorized by your HMO physician; however, these physicians are independent contractors and they see you in their own offices, side by side with their fee-for-service patients.

Because these plans are more loosely managed, costs run somewhat higher. Premiums tend to exceed those of group practice HMOs and may be comparable to those imposed by indemnity insurance. IPAs, however, offer more extensive benefits than the latter. People who wish to continue receiving care from their present physician may save money by joining an IPA in which that physician is enrolled.

Preferred Provider Insurance

This type of plan—unlike HMO coverage—allows you to choose between restricted and unrestricted coverage each time you need care. You may use the services of a designated group of providers (physicians, hospitals, and other medical professionals and services) or receive care from providers and hospitals not included on the list and pay a financial penalty for doing so. In some cases, the designated providers, called "preferred providers," form a Preferred Provider Organization (PPO) that contracts with a number of insurers or employers. In other cases, the designated providers have come together in a less formal grouping called a Preferred Provider Arrangement or a Preferred Provider Association (PPA).

Because most of these organizations are quite loosely structured, they do not "manage" your care the way an HMO does. Most or all of the cost-saving comes from the discounts that the preferred providers offer your employer or insurance company. Premiums tend to be similar to those set by indemnity insurers, but the coverage is much more extensive for those who receive care from the preferred providers. The 1987 business survey found that 11 percent of employees were enrolled in preferred provider plans; that figure, too, is expected to double by the early 1990s.

AT&T is planning to eliminate its indemnity plan in 1991 and substitute preferred provider insurance. Employees who choose preferred providers will pay a $150 deductible, 5 to 10 percent of most charges, and nothing for hospitalization, compared with a $200 deductible and 20 percent of all covered benefits if they go outside the preferred list.

Other Care-Managing Strategies

To reduce expenses, companies are seeking ways to simplify their health insurance programs. But while HMOs have been more successful than indemnity and PPO plans in keeping premium costs down, most employers want to offer at least one insurance plan that offers unrestricted freedom of choice.

However, that freedom may be too expensive for employees to consider as a real alternative. An example is the case of Allied-Signal (a national employer with headquarters in Morristown, New Jersey), which signed a three-year contract with CIGNA, a large insurance company, to be its exclusive provider of several different types of health insurance: a CIGNA indemnity insurance plan, a CIGNA preferred provider option, and a number of CIGNA-run HMOs of various models. CIGNA offered strong financial incentives to choose one of its HMOs and covered those who enrolled almost in full for most services. Those who chose indemnity insurance for their family plan had a deductible level set at 3 percent of their base salary ($600 for those who earned $20,000 a year) and were responsible for 20 percent of their covered medical expenses after meeting the deductible. For many, the indemnity alternative proved prohibitively expensive.

Some HMOs have created plans called "Self-Referral Option (SRO) HMOs" or "Point-of-Service" HMOs. If you sign up for one of these plans, you can either receive care from physicians and hospitals approved by the plan and enjoy full benefits, or go outside the HMO and pay a financial penalty, such as having to meet a deductible and/or pay co-insurance.

Reducing Costs: Government Initiatives

Through its funding of Medicare (for those over sixty-five), Medicaid (for the poor), and health insurance programs for federal employees and the military, the federal government is by far the largest health care payer in the United States. Because of this sheer size, governmental health insurance decisions have far-reaching effects and influence the kinds of coverage everyone else receives.

The federal government has attempted to reduce Medicare costs by encouraging beneficiaries to use HMOs and Competitive Medical Plans (CMPs). CMPs operate similarly to HMOs, though they are not as tightly regulated, and they are organized to service the Medicare market exclusively. Current budget proposals include reducing Medicare Part B premiums by 20 percent for those beneficiaries who enroll in HMOs or CMPs and increasing Medicaid funding to states that up their enrollments of Medicaid recipients in managed care plans. More and more federal employees are opting for HMO membership to avoid costly indemnity premiums.

The Department of Defense is experimenting with a program in California and Hawaii that encourages military dependents and retirees covered by the Civilian Health and Medical Program for the Uniformed Services (CHAMPUS) to use managed care systems. CHAMPUS beneficiaries in those states can enroll in an HMO (CHAMPUS Prime) and receive all their care from its providers while paying only small co-payments, or they can choose a preferred provider system (CHAMPUS Extra) and pay lower co-insurance when care is delivered by network physicians and hospitals. The

Department has asked Congress to extend this pilot program to Arizona, Nevada, and New Mexico.

The Federal Government Puts a Lid on Hospital Stays

In 1983, the government made a decision that has had vast consequences. It looked at the tremendous hospital costs being generated by Medicare patients and decided to stop reimbursing hospitals on a "cost-based" system—with the hospitals submitting bills and the government paying them. Instead, it switched to a "Prospective Payment System" (PPS). Now, when a Medicare patient is discharged from a hospital, his or her case is assigned to one of several hundred categories called "Diagnosis Related Groups," or DRGs, and the hospital is given a lump-sum payment that the government has predetermined is appropriate for that particular diagnostic category.

This change turned hospital incentives upside down. Formerly, the longer the stay, the more the hospital earned; not surprisingly, people often stayed in the hospital longer than was medically necessary. Now, because hospitals are paid the same flat fee regardless of the length of stay, they make more money by getting Medicare patients out as soon as possible, or "quicker and sicker," as critics of the system put it. DRGs, however, did not control total costs—just inpatient costs. Hospital administrators quickly learned that many surgical procedures could be performed safely in hospital outpatient departments, where the new regulations did not apply. This shift to increased outpatient care has contributed significantly to the continued rapid increase in Medicare costs.

Other Medicare restrictions did help the government manage its costs. Maximum allowable charges put a lid on reimbursement for physicians' fees. Mandatory lab assignment rules regulated charges for tests. Late in 1989, Congress passed legislation that will, by the mid-1990s, significantly change the way Medicare reimburses physicians (see page 176).

Trade-Offs: Which Plan Is Best for You?

Unrestricted freedom of choice has long been a watchword of organized medicine—and valued by many consumers—but as business and government expand their efforts to control health care costs, it may well come at a high price. Buyers of health insurance must now make trade-offs. The trick is to know what the trade-offs are and how they will affect you. You may decide that you want complete freedom of choice each time you need medical care; if so, indemnity insurance, even if it is more expensive, will be the best answer for you. If you travel extensively, you may decide to look for a plan that allows you to make decisions wherever and whenever the need arises, even if the coverage is not as extensive. If you have moved to a new city, you may feel somewhat daunted by the prospect of making good choices from a cityful of doctors; if so, you may accept a health plan with a limited list of doctors if the plan has a reputation for high quality. If you are starting a family, you may be most interested in a plan that offers extensive coverage for the costs of pregnancy and the care of newborns and infants; if such a plan has restrictions in other areas, these may be worth the trade-off.

This book is designed to help you make truly informed choices. It will teach you how to read and understand insurance terminology, how to evaluate and compare the true financial worth of the various plans you are offered, and how to assess the impact on your health care of the rules that a given type of plan contains.

As you learn about the different kinds of health insurance plans available to you, bear in mind that the type of plan you choose may affect the *way* you get your health care. After reading about your insurance options, you will find a chapter that discusses the basic principles of good medical care. Armed with this information, you will be able to understand how the insurance plans you are considering may affect your ability to get good health care.

1

Indemnity Insurance: Where It Came from and How It Works

Indemnity insurance is a form of coverage that pays predetermined amounts of money for defined services. Until 1980, indemnity health insurance plans covered most insured people in this country, other than those who were eligible for Medicare or Medicaid. In the past, "indemnity" described a specific kind of contract—one that promised to reimburse you a fixed dollar amount toward certain medical expenses that you incurred. For example, you might have subscribed to an indemnity plan that paid you $100 for each day you spent in the hospital. You would first pay the hospital whatever it charged for your stay and then submit your bill to the company for the $100-per-day reimbursement.

Although some people buy a fixed-dollar policy to supplement their regular plan, this type of coverage is no longer offered as basic health insurance. Nevertheless, the term "indemnity" has remained. Today, it commonly refers to a policy that covers your medical expenses according to a given formula and allows you to choose any licensed physician or accredited hospital. (In the absence of a mandate by the state, indemnity plans usually offer minimal reimbursement, if any, for care given by nontraditional providers such as chiropractors, homeopaths, and naturopaths. Many states have mandated coverage for chiropractic services.) And nowadays, rather than paying all your expenses first, you can usually arrange for the physician or hospital to be paid directly by your insurance, leaving you responsible for paying only the portion of the bill that is not covered.

A Brief History of Indemnity Insurance

In 1929 a group of schoolteachers in Dallas, Texas, contracted with Baylor University to provide them with up to twenty-one days of hospital care a year for a monthly premium of fifty cents. Hospitals around the country, struggling with a shortage of funds and increasing bad debt, were quick to see the advantage of the hospitalization insurance that Baylor was providing, and the idea spread rapidly. All these hospital-based insurance plans were eventually subsumed under what is still the largest provider of indemnity insurance, the Blue Cross and Blue Shield Association. (The now-familiar "blue cross" symbol originated with the Minnesota Hospital Services Association.)

Plans that offered coverage for physicians' fees took root in the West and spread to the rest of the United States. Since the early part of this century, a handful of physicians' groups, particularly in the state of Washington, had been offering insurance coverage for their services, but it was not until the early 1940s, with the establishment of the first Blue Shield plan, in California, that the concept of coverage for physicians' services caught on nationwide. Although Blue Cross and Blue Shield plans were structured as independent not-for-profit companies, they often joined forces for administrative and marketing purposes, and the "Blues," as they are now commonly called, have had a powerful influence on the development of health insurance in this country and on the expectations of those who buy and use insurance.

Key Characteristics of a Blue Cross/Blue Shield Policy

The Blue Cross concept originated during an era of relatively low medical costs, and the way policies were structured suited the times and distinguished the Blues from their competitors: commercial for-profit insurance companies like Prudential, Travelers, and Aetna. Although specific plans varied somewhat, they all contained the same key features, and some of these features have been adopted by modern indemnity plans.

Service benefits. Payment was made in full for specific services rather than with specified amounts toward the costs of those services. For example, a Blue Cross plan would cover in *full* ninety days of room and board in a semiprivate hospital room; by contrast, a commercial indemnity insurance plan would pay *a certain number of dollars per day* for up to ninety days.

First dollar coverage. Blue Cross policies paid for coverage beginning on *the first day* of hospitalization instead of requiring policyholders to pay a certain amount of money toward their expenses before they were eligible to apply for reimbursement.

Provider contracts. Special contractual and pricing relationships were signed with the hospitals and physicians that provided care to those covered by the plans. Contracted doctors, or "participating physicians," as they were called, agreed to accept the Blues' reimbursement as full payment for services, and members who used them were thus protected from excess billing.

Community rating. Health insurance was provided to everyone in a given state or region regardless of age, sex, geographic area, or utilization of medical services.

These features were attractive to consumers. Payment in full for hospital rooms meant freedom from any financial burden; so did first dollar coverage. Because hospitals and physicians often billed the plan directly, patients did not have to lay out sums of money and submit claim forms. By negotiating substantial discounts with physicians and hospitals, the Blues were usually able to offer insurance at a lower cost than their commercial competitors.

But commercial carriers found a new niche in the medical insurance market by adding to the traditional rating factors of age, sex, and geographic area a different type of actuarial calculation called "experience rating." Premiums were based on how much it cost to pay for medical care for employees in a given company; therefore, companies with healthier than average employees were charged lower rates than the Blues could offer.

Major Medical Plans

Until the 1960s, people spent almost all of their health care dollars on hospitals and physicians. Therefore, insurance that covered only these two areas was adequate. But as laboratory tests, X rays, and drugs became more sophisticated and more effective, they began to play an expanded role in medical practice, and consumers found themselves paying substantial sums for care that their policies did not cover. In response, both the Blues and commercial insurers developed additional components to their coverage and termed their new programs *major medical plans.* Major medical plans generally featured a deductible amount that had to be paid by the insured person before he or she could apply for reimbursement, and a formula for coverage once the deductible was met: for example, 80 percent of covered charges up to a maximum of $20,000.

At this point, health insurance was a cumbersome product with three different components (hospital, physician, and major medical), sometimes administered through two or three different companies, each with its own assorted rules and deductibles. Policyholders often had to go through an elaborate process in order to be reimbursed. They would submit all their laboratory bills to the company that provided hospital coverage, wait for them to be rejected, and only then submit them to the major medical plan, where the claims ought to have gone in the first place.

Commercial insurers took advantage of this confusion to offer a more streamlined product: the *comprehensive major medical plan.* This type of plan provided combined coverage for hospital, physician, drugs, lab tests, X rays, and other procedures. It featured a single deductible and called for the insured person to pay a certain percentage (usually 10 or 20 percent) of the bills up to a specified ceiling ($2,000 was a typical amount). After that, the insurance company provided 100 percent coverage up to a high maximum (usually $250,000 or more).

Comprehensive indemnity plans became very attractive to employers. They were easy to explain and to administer, and eventually commercial insurance companies gained an edge over the Blues, who were reluctant to part with the concept of first dollar coverage and unable to untangle the administrative complexities that precluded a simpler and more unified type of plan.

But employer-sponsored insurance would not be the popular product it is today without a crucial decision made by the federal government in 1943, when the Internal Revenue Service ruled that employers' contributions to employee health insurance were exempt from taxable income. This decision encouraged workers to bargain for substantial—and untaxed—enhancements to their health insurance, as opposed to taxable salary increases, and led to a tremendous increase both in the breadth of coverage offered by employers and in the percentage of working people who were covered by a health insurance policy.

Problems with Indemnity Insurance

The problems we as a country now face in attempting to provide affordable health insurance are rooted in much earlier decisions. From the beginning, the design of indemnity insurance plans contained weaknesses that now undermine our ability to control health care expenditures.

The typical indemnity plan offered consumers free choice of physicians, with no inducement to use those whose fees were lower or whose style of practice was more cost-conscious. Commercial insurance carriers sold and administered insurance; they did not have relationships with physicians and could not control their fees. Workers pushed for improvements in health insurance coverage, and insurance plans continued to become more comprehensive and more expensive.

Neither patients nor physicians have had any incentive to save money under this system, so the costs of health insurance to employers have continued to mount. Indemnity insurance providers, in order to offer free choice of physicians and hospitals, have had to raise premiums substantially and have sought to control expenses by the various cost-cutting and cost-shifting measures we identified in the Introduction. When coverage and cost to the insured are taken together, most indemnity plans offered nowadays offer less protection. Whereas the range of benefits may be comprehensive, larger deductibles pose a financial barrier to needed care. And when extensive care is required, the insured will likely encounter high out-of-pocket expenses.

A Short Course in Indemnity Insurance

If you are planning to buy an indemnity policy, you should be prepared to study its provisions, keep careful records, and submit claim forms for all the medical bills that it covers. To make an informed choice of an indemnity plan, you will need to evaluate the plan's provisions and estimate how they apply to your particular situation.

Suppose, for example, that an insurance company we'll call Mutual Providential of Hartford offers the following indemnity policy. For a monthly premium of $300, your family of four will be protected from the expenses of illness or accident. Benefits will include coverage for hospital costs, physicians' fees, and laboratory tests, as well as X rays, EKGs, and other diagnostic procedures. Screening tests, routine checkups, and a number of other medical services are not covered. Before being able to claim benefits, each family member will have to satisfy a $200 deductible. Beyond the deductible, each family member will pay co-insurance of 20 percent on subsequent covered expenses up to a stop-loss of $3,000. To help you understand the provisions of this policy, we'll explain each one in turn.

Premium

If you are employed, your employer will generally pay some of the premium. In the past, many employers paid the full cost; now there is a trend toward requiring an employee contribution. The Wyatt Company surveys a large number of employees regularly to follow these trends. The company's Compare Database shows that late in 1989 more than three-quarters of employers required employee contributions toward medical plans. Employees generally paid no more than $15 a month for single coverage and $30 to $100 a month toward a family plan. If your employer offers you a choice of plans, your premium contribution may be higher if the plan you choose is more expensive for your employer to provide.

Deductible

The deductible is an amount of money you pay toward the covered medical expenses you incur in a given calendar year *before* you become eligible for insurance benefits. This sum has increased dramatically in the last few years. Wyatt's Compare Database shows that 70 percent of comprehensive indemnity plans had deductibles of $100 or less in 1984; by the end of 1989, 50 percent of plans had deductibles of $150 or more for individuals and $300 or more for families. Employers may raise deductibles to help keep premium increases down.

To satisfy a deductible, you must spend the amount the plan specifies out of your own pocket—and you must spend it on the types of services the plan covers. If you have only one doctor's bill for $60 for the entire year, and your deductible is $100, you will not receive any money in reimbursement. If, however, you incur a second bill of $60, you will have spent a total of $120 on office visits. You have now exceeded the deductible by $20, and that amount may be reimbursable—*may* be reimbursable, because there are a few other conditions that must be met. If, for example, the office visits were for preventive care, such as well-child visits to a pediatrician, and if your plan does not cover preventive care, these expenses cannot be used to satisfy a deductible. Some plans offer an advantage by exempting certain types of expenses from the deductible requirement (for instance, the costs of hospitalization or drugs).

It's a good idea to recheck the deductible at each of your employer's open enrollment periods—usually annually. Ask yourself each time whether you might hesitate to see a doctor because you had not yet satisfied the deductible for the year. If you would forgo care, you should consider switching to a managed health care plan (a PPO or an HMO) that does not require you to pay a deductible before you have coverage.

Family Deductible

To offer larger families some extra protection, most family policies contain one deductible amount per person and another, higher, amount per family. The family deductible is usually set at either two or three times the individual deductible; a typical example would be $100 (individual)/$300 (family).

Because the concept of a family deductible is a confusing one, you might find it helpful to visualize the steps you would take to meet it. Suppose you decide to buy a Mutual Providential policy with a $100/$300 deductible to cover your family of five. Your coverage begins on January 1, and you want to know when you have satisfied the family deductible of $300.

Imagine that each family member who receives care for a covered medical expense writes the amount on a slip of paper and tosses it into a pot. For example, Dad has a $60 office visit—a covered expense—in January. He pays for it out of pocket, writes $60 on a slip of paper, and puts it in the pot. A few days later, he returns for a follow-up visit at $40—also covered—and he pays for that. He writes $40 on the slip and tosses it in the pot. He has now satisfied his *individual* deductible ($100), and any care that he himself receives from now until the end of the year—as long as it is covered—will be reimbursable to the extent provided by the policy. He cannot, however, apply any more of the expenses he incurs toward satisfying the family deductible.

Each family member who has medical expenses follows the same procedure, throwing a slip of paper with the amount spent into the pot until he or she satisfies the $100 individual deductible. Once the slips total $300, either by three family members reaching their $100 individual deductibles or by any combination of family members spending a total of $300—as long as no single member contributes more than $100—the family deductible is satisfied for that year.

Multiple Deductibles

The typical insurance policy contains a single deductible. Once you have satisfied it, the plan will reimburse you for your expenses up to the limits of the policy. Some policies, however, require you to satisfy a separate deductible for each new type of charge, each new diagnosis, each hospital admission, each hospital emergency room visit, or each month the policy is in force. Termed a "per cause" or "per condition" deductible, this approach is rarely in your interest.

Covered Benefits

These are the services for which you will be reimbursed. If you are choosing a plan offered by your employer, you will receive material listing what benefits are covered; if you are buying your own insurance, you can read a copy of the policy before you purchase it.

According to The Wyatt Company, which has a database covering one out of every seven people who receive health insurance through an employer, as of 1990 almost all comprehensive indemnity plans cover hospital charges, surgical fees, physician fees for hospital care and office care, emergency room fees, and ambulatory facility charges. Ninety-five percent of them cover outpatient diagnostic tests such as laboratory tests, X rays, EKGs, and other types of diagnostic procedures (for example, EEGs, nuclear medicine, and ultrasound).

Although most plans cover hospitalization for mental illness, almost all impose one or more limitations—for instance, on the number of inpatient days, the number of confinements, the total dollars paid in a given year, or the total dollars paid in a lifetime. Virtually all indemnity plans limit outpatient psychotherapy. They may restrict the number of visits, dollars paid per visit, or total dollars spent on treatment.

Home health care is covered to some extent by 86 percent of policies, hospice care by 78 percent, and chemical dependency by 68 percent. The incidence of coverage for preventive care is considerably less: only 38 percent of policies cover periodic physical exams and 29 percent cover health screening. Prescription drugs are usually covered to some extent, but reimbursement for eye exams and glasses is highly variable. When you are calculating what you expect to be reimbursed by your insurance plan, remember that the only expenses you can include are those for covered benefits.

Co-Insurance

This term refers to the percentage of covered medical costs you will continue to pay toward the expenses you incur after you have satisfied the deductible. You and your partner, the insurance company, agree to split the costs according to a predetermined ratio, with the company paying the higher percentage. The most common arrangement has been an 80/20 split, with the company paying 80 percent of your covered costs and you paying 20 percent. (A number of employers provide indemnity insurance plans with a preferred provider option. In this case, you will be rewarded with a better co-insurance rate if you use physicians and services from the preferred list.)

How does this co-insurance work in actual numbers? Our fictitious Mutual Providential plan has a $100 deductible and an 80/20 co-insurance rate. If you have paid out $120 in physician fees, you are now eligible to be reimbursed.

physician fees	=	$120
amount of deductible	=	$100
amount of money above deductible	=	$20
80% to be paid by insurance plan	=	$16
20% you will pay as co-insurance	=	$ 4

This example, however, does not take into account another twist in insurers' definitions of what they will pay as their share of total expenses—the usual, customary, and reasonable restrictions.

UCR (Usual, Customary, and Reasonable)

In order to protect the insurance company from paying what it considers excessive physician bills, almost all indemnity policies restrict coverage to "UCR"—"usual, customary, and reasonable" fees.

Usual:	What a specific physician charges patients
Customary:	What most physicians in your community charge
Reasonable:	A maximum fee set by the insurance company

Each insurance company sets its own specific UCR guidelines, then pays the physician's *usual* fee unless that fee exceeds the *customary* fee that physicians in that community charge for a particular service. In actual practice, these guidelines are often more arbitrary than the words "usual," "customary," and "reasonable" would seem to imply. If you believe that you are not being reimbursed to the full extent of the policy, discuss the matter with your physician. If your case was unusually complicated, he or she may request a review, and your insurance company may agree that the physician's higher fee was *reasonable.*

UCR guidelines can vary significantly. Some insurance companies base their customary levels on the fee patterns of all physicians in a community, whereas others differentiate by specialty. Thus, they may pay a higher fee to a general surgeon than to a family physician for the same procedure. Some companies use regional or statewide averages; others keep a claims-history file on each physician.

Here's how UCR guidelines can affect the way you are reimbursed for physicians' fees. Suppose your first physician's bill of the year is for a hysterectomy, and your gynecologist charges you $2,000 for the procedure. You know that you have to meet your $100 deductible, but you assume the remainder of the bill will be reimbursed at the 80 percent co-insurance rate that Mutual Providential promised you. Your calculation of your expected reimbursement looks like this:

physician's fee =	$2,000
deductible that you will pay =	$ 100
fee minus $100 deductible =	$1,900
80% (of $1,900) that Mutual Providential will pay =	$1,520
20% co-insurance that you will pay =	$ 380

Instead of a bill for $480 (a $100 deductible plus 20 percent co-insurance) that you expected to pay, you receive a statement from your physician informing you that your insurance company has paid $1,120 toward the fee and that you now owe a total of $880.

When you call your insurance company to have the matter set straight, the clerk explains that everything is in order and according to their arithmetic, the proper calculation is as follows:

UCR physician's fee for hysterectomy = $1,500
fee minus $100 deductible that you pay = $1,400
80% (of $1,400) that Mutual Providential will pay = $1,120

Find out *before* you sign up for a health insurance plan what kinds of fee limitations exist, and make sure they are in line for your particular community and for the doctors you would be likely to use. Otherwise, an unfavorable UCR reimbursement like the one above may, in effect, turn the 80/20 co-insurance split into a 50/50 partnership, hardly what you had in mind when you bought the policy.

Insurance companies do not publish their UCR guidelines, but they will give you a figure for a specific procedure done by a particular physician if you ask. Because UCR rates are based on each individual doctor's past pattern of billing, or "fee profile," insurance companies give out actual numbers only on a claim-by-claim basis.

Indemnity Fee Schedule (Maximum Fee Schedule)

Some insurers, especially those without much business in a given community, use a fee schedule that is based neither on *usual* nor on *customary* charges. Instead, they set maximum amounts they will reimburse for each type of service and procedure. Their schedule may be generous enough to cover most fees in full or so meager that it effectively nullifies the 80/20 co-insurance split the policy was supposed to cover—forcing the insured to carry a far heavier burden of expense. Pay special attention to a policy's surgical fee schedule, and check with local physicians to see whether the sums for specific procedures sound reasonable before you commit to a policy with a maximum fee schedule.

Stop-Loss

This feature protects you from catastrophically large expenses by placing an annual ceiling on the co-insurance amount you will have to pay toward *covered* medical expenses. After a policyholder reaches the stop-loss ceiling, the insurance company will pay 100 percent of covered hospital and physicians' bills (subject to that company's UCR schedules). Your insurance company might be willing to stretch the rules a bit if you suffered a severe injury in December and were still hospitalized and incurring expenses for that injury in January. Most stop-loss figures are set in the $2,500 to $5,000 range, but some employers recalculate the stop-loss annually as a percentage of the subscriber's salary.

The stop-loss is the most important feature of your health care insurance in protecting you against the kinds of medical expenses that could wipe you out financially. Without it, you do not have any protection against catastrophic expenses. According to the Wyatt survey, more than 80 percent of employers provide a stop-loss in the indemnity policies offered to their employees.

If possible, make sure that the plan you select has a reasonable ceiling. Cardiac surgery can cost $20,000 or more. Bills for a sick premature baby can exceed $100,000. Without stop-loss protection, you would have to pay 20 percent or more in co-insurance.

Let's look at how the stop-loss provision works. Suppose your first medical expense of the year was a hospital bill of $1,650 for a two-day stay plus $950 in physicians' bills, none of which exceeded the UCR. Your Mutual Providential plan has a $2,500 stop-loss. How much of the bill will you pay?

total bill	=	$2,600
bill minus $100 deductible	=	$2,500
20% (of $2,500) co-insurance that you will pay	=	$ 500
your total out-of-pocket expense (deductible plus co-insurance)	=	$ 600

Because your total bill of $2,600 (minus the $100 deductible) equals your stop-loss ceiling, any further covered expenses that do not exceed the UCR should be fully reimbursed by the insurance plan.

Suppose that your medical problem was not treated in the hospital but instead required a series of ten office visits and two office procedures. If you are not cautious about the fee schedule your insurance plan uses, you might find that your stop-loss gives you far less protection than you assumed. Suppose that your Mutual Providential plan allows $75 for each office visit and $500 for each procedure. What would you pay in this situation?

Your physician's bill:

10 office visits at $100 each	=	$1,000
2 procedures at $800 each	=	$1,600
total bill	=	$2,600

Reimbursement by insurance plan:

10 visits at $75 each	=	$ 750
2 procedures at $500 each	=	$1,000
subtotal	=	$1,750
minus $100 deductible	=	$1,650
co-insurance (80% of $1,650) total	=	$1,320

Your out-of-pocket expenses would be $1,280 ($2,600 less $1,320). The insurance company followed its UCR guidelines in calculating what it would reimburse. Under its rules, it agreed to pay only $75 toward the visits for which your doctor billed you $100. The stop-loss applies only to covered benefits. Hence, $25 of each office visit is not covered and therefore cannot be counted toward the stop-loss; similarly, $300 of each procedure is not covered and is not applied toward the stop-loss.

Even though the total amount of the physician's bills is identical to the total amount of the bills generated by the hospitalization, you have only reached $1,650 of your stop-loss. Not only will you have to pay the $1,280, which is not reimbursed by insurance in this instance, but the next $850 of allowed expense during the year will still be subject to co-insurance. Therefore, you will pay an additional $170 before reaching your stop-loss.

Lifetime Maximum

A stop-loss protects *you* by placing a cap on the amount you must pay in a given year; a lifetime maximum protects *the insurance company* by putting a ceiling on the amount it will pay toward your medical expenses over your lifetime. Most plans have lifetime maximums between $250,000 and $1 million. The Wyatt Company found that only 8 percent of plans offered by employers have lower maximums. Certain plans replenish some of the amount you have used up each year.

Once you are up to the limit, many plans will not allow you to buy further coverage; the only way you could continue to be insured at that point would be to change insurance carriers. If your employer does not offer a choice of plans, you would have to change employers in order to subscribe to group insurance. You would not be able to buy your own individual coverage; someone sick enough to use up a lifetime maximum could not pass the health screening that nongroup policies require.

A lifetime maximum hurts those who most need insurance and, in our opinion, contradicts the whole purpose of insurance: to protect the individual from financial catastrophe. Practically speaking, however, this limitation affects very few subscribers, since the probability of reaching such a limit is extraordinarily low.

Exclusions

Pay careful attention to the exclusions in the policies you are considering and ask questions *before* you sign up. Each plan will specify those medical services it does not cover. Many plans exclude "care that is not medically necessary to treat a disease." If your policy contains a similar phrase, it will exclude preventive care and routine check-ups.

Two areas that may cause confusion deserve your careful attention: coverage for surgery and coverage for mental illness. Most insurers exclude surgery that is purely cosmetic, but you may encounter some variations. Some companies do not believe that surgical treatment of obesity is safe or effective, and they refuse to cover it; others will cover it under certain circumstances. Surgery for various jaw and/or dental problems is apt to be treated differently by different companies. Even the coverage offered by one company for such problems may vary from one time to another. For example, one company included in its coverage the repair of natural teeth injured in an accident. However, when it denied the claim of a man who broke an already decayed tooth while biting an apple and had the denial overruled by a court, it changed its policies to exclude all dental services.

Coverage for mental illness often has limitations. Specific illnesses, such as schizophrenia or anorexia nervosa, may be excluded, and reimbursement for psychotherapy will usually carry limitations. In addition, coverage of treatment for chemical dependency can vary greatly from one plan to another.

Some plans limit the duration of therapy or the number of visits. Or they may cover only one visit a month for a given emotional problem. Such a limitation leaves you financially exposed if your problem is serious and you are unable to wait a month for a follow-up visit.

Sometimes coverage depends on whether a given problem has physical consequences. Congenital defects that cause physical problems are generally covered but not those that cause only psychological problems.

Procedures that involve reshaping normal breasts or restoring breasts after mastectomy seem to be a particular source of controversy. Some states have passed laws requiring the coverage of breast reconstruction following mastectomy. Even in those states, however, insurance plans may still refuse to pay for reduction of the normal breast to match the one that has had surgery. Reduction mammoplasty (a procedure used to reduce the size of unusually large breasts) may be covered in the presence of certain physical symptoms (back pain, for example) or evidence of severity (indentations by bra straps); some companies may take into account the psychological distress that a woman with unusually large breasts may suffer.

Experimental and investigational procedures, controversial procedures, and very expensive new procedures are often subject to exclusions. Many policies do not cover the following:

- certain transplant procedures such as pancreas, heart/lung, and multiple organs
- liver transplants, except for those that meet certain criteria
- surgery or other invasive treatments for obesity
- therapeutic abortion
- extensive medical work-ups for infertility
- expenses in connection with *in vitro* fertilization
- expenses for surrogate mothers
- routine circumcision
- treatment of certain jaw problems, particularly of the temporo-mandibular joint (TMJ syndrome)

Preexisting Conditions (PECs)

Some insurance plans will not pay for treatment of medical problems that existed before you signed up, even though those conditions are covered if they occur after you become a subscriber. Small employers, because they have difficulty buying affordable insurance, are most apt to offer plans with these restrictions.

Some policies may reimburse PECs at a lower rate than other problems, and some policies may begin to pay for treatment after a certain time period has elapsed. You might decide to buy a policy that requires you to wait six months for a hernia repair, if your doctor agrees that a delay would do no harm.

Pay attention not only to the actual conditions that are excluded from coverage but also to the exact way in which their "preexistence" is established. Some policies define a PEC as a medical problem that has been diagnosed or treated by a physician in the past year; others exclude conditions that you were aware of, whether or not you sought medical advice.

If an insurance plan contains PEC limitations, you will be required to fill out a medical form that asks questions about all your past and present medical conditions. Fill out the form honestly. Deliberate falsification of your medical history constitutes fraud, which, if discovered, will result in your losing all your health insurance coverage.

Co-Payment

A co-payment is a fixed amount that you pay when you use a service—not to be confused with co-insurance, which is a percentage. For example, some insurance plans require you to make a co-payment of $100 or $200 for each hospital admission. Co-payments are frequently a feature of a prescription drug insurance plan that is separate from your company's main insurance plan.

Major Medical

Most indemnity plans provide coverage for hospitalization and other medical expenses; such plans are called "comprehensive plans." Some employers, however, offer a two-part indemnity package: a *base* plan, which covers hospitalization, and sometimes surgical fees, in full, and a *major medical* plan, which supplements the base plan by covering physician fees and other services such as X rays, laboratory work, and prescription drugs. Major medical plans, like comprehensive indemnity plans, specify a deductible and a co-insurance rate.

Some major medical plans do not offer the protection of a stop-loss.

High-Option Plans and Low-Option Plans

Some companies offer employees the choice of paying higher rates for fuller medical coverage. A high-option plan offers broader benefits and is considerably more expensive than a low-option plan; it is the insurance equivalent of the "fully loaded" automobile. With a high-option plan, you will have a lower deductible, a more favorable co-insurance rate (80 percent), and a greater number of covered benefits, such as pharmacy and vision care. The low-option plan offers a stripped-down, no-frills insurance vehicle with a higher deductible, less favorable co-insurance (70 percent), and fewer covered benefits. This choice of plans is often a feature of "flexible benefits" programs. Flexible benefits programs give employees the opportunity to design their own benefits packages, up to a certain dollar limit. These programs usually have two components: a "core" group of benefits (for example, medical insurance and dental insurance) and additional optional benefits employees can select based on personal preference (perhaps life insurance, disability insurance, or dependent care). Often a low-option medical plan is included as a core benefit and a high-option plan as an optional benefit.

A low-option plan is appealing to healthy people who are willing to bet on their continuing good health. If you fit this category, you might save perhaps $20 a month in premium costs by choosing a low-option plan with a $500 deductible instead of a high-option one with a $100 deductible. If you win the bet, you are ahead $240 for the year. If you end up in a hospital emergency room after a serious accident, you will be responsible for the first $500 of your expenses in addition to co-insurance. (See pages 38–39 for a further discussion of low-option plans for people who buy their own insurance.)

Dual Coverage

If you are married, and if both you and your spouse are eligible for insurance through your employers, you may have a significant financial advantage if each of you carries the other in your insurance. Depending on the particular policies you and your spouse choose, you may recover most of your medical expenses by listing each other on your health insurance policies. (For a detailed discussion of dual coverage, see pages 147–50.)

How to Calculate What a Policy Is Worth to You

To evaluate how much protection a given indemnity plan is likely to provide, you need to do four things:

1. Estimate the types and amounts of medical expenses you can reasonably expect.
2. Study the extent of coverage a particular policy offers for those expenses.
3. Know what limitations the policy places on your claims (UCR, PECs, stop-loss, etc.).
4. Decide how well the coverage fits your particular situation.

The only way you can find out how well a particular insurance plan will work for you is to plug in some numbers. What may look like a good deal in the sales literature for a policy or in the comparison of benefits handout your company gives you may in fact work against you.

Suppose, for instance, that you are offered a plan that eliminates the usual co-insurance formula and instead states the following: your deductible is $150, and you pay all the costs for the first visit for a particular medical problem; all subsequent visits for that problem will be covered in full. "Sounds good," you say, and you sign up.

Then you develop a medical problem. Your doctor does a thorough examination and orders some lab work. Cost: $125. Three follow-up visits cost $35 each. Total cost: $230. Your reimbursement: $00.00. Because you are responsible for the first visit, the $125 fee for your first visit cannot be applied to satisfy the deductible. The fees for the three subsequent visits add up to $105, not enough to satisfy your $150 deductible. What you didn't know or remember (but your insurer did), is that the first visit for a medical problem usually costs far more than subsequent visits. In addition, you may have equated paying out of pocket for the first visit with satisfying the deductible. In this example, the two provisions work entirely independently of each other—at your expense.

To avoid the pitfalls that await the unwary buyer, get out your insurance literature, sharpen your pencil, jot down some facts about the plan or plans you are considering, and be ready to ask questions of the insurance company's representative or your employer's benefits administrator until you're sure you understand each provision fully.

Make sure the policy has a stop-loss provision. This is one of the most important features of your policy. If there is no stop-loss, you are vulnerable to catastrophically large bills, perhaps large enough to wipe you out financially. Victims of serious auto accidents, premature babies, patients with brain hemorrhage or AIDS or cancer can incur huge medical bills. If you were to run up bills of $100,000 or more, an indemnity policy with a $100 deductible, 80 percent co-insurance, and a $5,000 stop-loss would cost you $1,100 in out-of-pocket expenses. The same plan with no stop-loss feature would cost you over $20,000.

Calculate your maximum out-of-pocket expense by adding the deductible to your co-insurance percentage of the stop-loss. This is the maximum amount of money you would be required to pay, as opposed to what the insurance company pays. Medical catastrophes are rare and unpredictable, but expenses in the range of $3,000 to $5,000 are less so. If you want to protect yourself against budget-breaking medical expenses, you will have to consider some upsetting possibilities.

Let's say you are pregnant or planning to become pregnant. If you have reason to believe you will need a cesarean section, you know that your expenses for childbirth may be considerable. If you have had serious heart problems recently, you are more apt to need expensive care in the next few years than would an entirely healthy person.

To calculate your maximum out-of-pocket expense for a given policy, add the deductible to your co-insurance percentage of the stop-loss. Our fictitious Mutual Providential policy has a $2,500 stop-loss and an 80/20 co-insurance rate:

20% of $2,500	=	$500
deductible	=	$100
total	=	$600

This calculation is worth doing, since the amounts may vary dramatically from policy to policy. Suppose that you are invited to choose one of the following three plans, each of which has one deductible for the year. The following calculation is for one person:

	Plan A	Plan B	Plan C
Deductible	$100	$200	$300
Co-insurance	80%	80%	75%
Stop-loss	$2,500	$3,000	$5,000
Maximum out-of-pocket expense	$600	$800	$1,550

Plan A has the lowest deductible and the lowest stop-loss. Chances are that its premium will be higher than the other two, and you must weigh the extra premium expense against the risk represented by the maximum amount you would have to spend out of your own funds. Naturally, that maximum may be considerably greater if you choose physicians who charge more than the insurance company's UCR schedule and if your policy does not cover preventive care. Plan C leaves you at the highest financial risk by far and should be considered only if its premium is substantially lower than that of the other two plans.

Once you have some sense of your total financial risk, you should calculate how well a given policy would cover the kinds of expenses you and your family are likely to incur. When you have determined this amount, you can use it to gauge how well any new indemnity policy would cover you.

Preferred Provider Insurance: The "No Lock-In" Alternative

In between the free choice offered by an indemnity policy and the restricted choice characteristic of a health maintenance organization lies an alternative: a plan that allows you unrestricted access to any licensed physician or accredited hospital while rewarding you financially for choosing from its approved list of physicians and hospitals. Preferred providers—physicians and other caregivers, pharmacies, hospitals, laboratories, and other medical services—may be selected because they provide care at a discount to plan members or because they have developed a cost-efficient style of medical care.

Such a plan adds a new wrinkle to traditional indemnity insurance by offering an opportunity to save money each time you seek medical care. Members of preferred provider plans who choose providers from the approved list are reimbursed in full or pay a very low rate of co-insurance—perhaps 10 percent. Members are free, at any time, to use the services of providers that are not on the list; that decision, however, comes at a price. They may have 90 to 100 percent coverage and no deductible to satisfy if they use preferred providers, as opposed to 60 to 80 percent coverage, with a deductible, if they use providers who do not appear on the preferred list. Some plans offer, as further incentives to use the preferred list, coverage for well-child care or for prescription drugs.

The PPO approach grew out of the needs of various groups: employers experiencing large increases in health care costs and insurance companies, hospitals, and physicians who were losing business to HMOs. Employers wanted to preserve choice and control costs. Insurance companies, hospitals, and physicians wanted to retain patients in a newly competitive health care market.

The phrase "preferred provider insurance" designates the whole plan—from the perspective of the consumer. You will see the letters "PPO" (Preferred Provider Organization) or sometimes "PPA" (Preferred Provider Association) used loosely to designate the same concept. These two acronyms actually refer to the providers and institutions on the approved list, who may have created a formal organization to represent their interests or may simply have signed a contract with a sponsoring organization such as an insurance company, a hospital, or an employer. Sometimes sponsoring organizations combine in a joint venture.

Until recently, there was no accreditation program for these groups, but in 1989 the American Association of Preferred Provider Organizations, in a joint venture with a private consulting firm, Medical Strategies, Incorporated, created an independent group, the American Accreditation Program, Incorporated (AAPI), to evaluate PPOs for accreditation. AAPI surveyors look for a comprehensive network of services on the preferred list. They consider how carefully physicians and hospitals are selected for their quality of care, whether there is a system to drop providers who give substandard care, whether the provider network has good financial controls, and whether it has appropriate systems to monitor quality of care and financial management.[1]

Both employers and employees find advantages in preferred provider insurance plans. Employers like the fact that these plans allow them to offer their employees better coverage at the same, or lower, cost. For example, General Hospital may agree to give a 20 percent discount on its services to a large employer. Now the employer can afford to offer an insurance plan that covers care at General Hospital in full.

Employees like preferred provider insurance because they retain full control to choose services and providers.

The "preferred" side of the plan may function in a number of different ways, and you will need to read the specific rules of the plan you are offered. Some plans require you to see a preferred primary care physician who must then approve any further care if you are to be reimbursed at the preferred rate. Others allow you to do your own picking and choosing from the approved list. The length of the list may vary; some plans may offer several hundred physicians and half a dozen hospitals.

Buying Your Own Health Insurance: Special Considerations

Whether you join a group insurance plan through an employer or sign up for a policy you find for yourself, the principles of buying indemnity insurance are the same. The difference, and it's a substantial one, is cost. Your main task will be to find health care insurance you can afford. To insure your family, you may have to spend $2,500 to $4,000 or more a year in premiums for a fairly comprehensive plan with a low deductible. Single people typically spend 40 percent of that figure to buy their own coverage.

For people who can afford these premiums, the primary consideration would be to buy the most comprehensive coverage with the best protection against catastrophic costs. If this is the case for you, compare Blue Cross/Blue Shield plans with those from well-established commercial carriers. Do the calculations we have recommended and select the plan that gives you the most for the money.

People on a tight budget, particularly those who are young and healthy, are sometimes tempted to do without health insurance. That option is a risky one.

Before you take that option, ask yourself the following questions:

- If I were to suffer a serious illness or injury, how would I pay my medical bills?
- If I were unable to pay large medical bills, how would I feel about ending up on Medicaid or filing for bankruptcy?
- Do I tend to worry about my health and to consult doctors for reassurance? Can I afford to do this without insurance?
- Do I want to be able to protect my financial assets in the event of a serious and expensive illness?
- Am I going to be self-employed for a number of years?
- How do I feel about the risk of not being able to buy individual insurance at some future time if I should develop a serious chronic condition such as diabetes, hypertension, or kidney disease?

The Low-Option Approach

If you can't or don't want to lay out large sums of money for premiums, you might decide to concentrate on the "catastrophic" aspect of insurance coverage and protect yourself only against the kinds of expenses you could never afford to pay yourself. Ask yourself first how much you can afford to pay for medical expenses out of your own pocket, and then how likely you are to incur those expenses.

Depending on where you live, rates may vary considerably, but the following table will give you some sense of how increasing the deductible can lower the premium. The monthly premium figures are for buyers who are between the ages of thirty and thirty-four. (These are the premiums charged to individuals by Blue Cross of Washington and Alaska in 1989.)

MONTHLY/ANNUAL PREMIUMS AT INCREASING DEDUCTIBLE LEVELS

Deductible	Single	Couple	Family
$200	$91/$1,092	$183/$2,196	$247/$2,964
$500	$73/$876	$146/$1,752	$197/$2,364
$1,000	$59/$708	$117/$1,404	$158/$1,896

As you see, you can save substantially on premiums if you are prepared to accept a large deductible. A family of four that used little health care in a year would spend $1,068 less a year if they took on a $1,000 deductible. (These deductible figures are for individuals; there may be a family deductible as well.) Make sure that any plan you buy has a stop-loss level you can live with, and then look for a plan with the highest deductible that you could afford if you had to begin paying for medical care.

Pointers for the Cautious Buyer

Buy insurance while you are healthy. If you wait until you are seriously ill, you may encounter exorbitant rates or exclusions for the very problem you most need covered.

Review insurance policies with great care. Pay special attention to exclusions and limitations. Also, find out under what circumstances your coverage can be canceled. You will be best off with a plan that can be canceled only if the company is discontinuing all individual policies.

Try to find an advantage. If you do not smoke, look for a plan that has lower premiums for nonsmokers. If you are over fifty years old, find out whether a Blue Cross plan would be a better buy than a commercial plan. As of mid-1990, Blue Cross plans in New York, Pennsylvania, Michigan, and Washington, D.C., were still community rated; this rating approach generally benefits older people. Women under age 55 are statistically more expensive to care for than men in that age group and therefore may also save money by buying a community-rated plan from Blue Cross.

Buy insurance as an individual only after you've exhausted all possibilities for group coverage. Investigate organizations you belong to, and those you might join, to see if they offer group insurance. Your college alumni association, a professional association in your field, or (if you are the owner of a business) your chamber of commerce may offer good coverage at a reasonable price. But if you have a serious medical condition, read the rules carefully. Policies purchased from these kinds of groups commonly contain restrictions for preexisting conditions.

Ask about payment schedules. You may be able to save money arranging to pay for your premium on an annual or a quarterly basis instead of paying month by month.

Make sure any policy you are considering is offered by a financially stable and reputable company. Best's Insurance Reports, a reference available in most libraries, is published annually by the A. M. Best Company, an independent company that has rated the financial strength of insurance companies for more than eighty years. Best rates companies as A+ (superior), A (Excellent), B+ (Very Good), C+ (Fairly Good), and C (Fair). Companies not rated are listed as NA (not assigned).

To formulate its ratings, Best evaluates a number of the companies' key financial indicators (profitability, use of debt, liquidity, adequacy of reserves, company management, etc.) based on information supplied by the companies themselves.

When using Best's ratings to evaluate a company's financial health, be sure of what company will actually issue the policy you're considering. Sometimes large companies with high Best ratings will use their name to market policies that will be issued through one of their subsidiaries, which may have a lower Best rating. You may be more comfortable buying a policy from a subsidiary whose parent company is rated A+ or A by Best, but that is by no means a guarantee of the subsidiary's financial strength.

Indeed, Best's ratings in no way guarantee that a high rated company won't have financial difficulties, or that a lower rated company will necessarily fail. But our advice is to seek out companies rated A+ or A and avoid any rated lower than B+. Blue Cross and Blue Shield, as nonprofit organizations, are not rated by Best.

If You Lose Your Group Coverage

If you are laid off, fired, planning to leave your job, or are for any reason about to lose your employer-provided insurance, one of your first concerns should be to continue your group health insurance coverage as long as possible. A law passed in 1985 will help you. This law (part of the Consolidated Omnibus Budget Reconciliation Act, or COBRA) requires your employer to offer you the option of continuing in the group plan for eighteen to thirty-six months (depending on a number of conditions) at your own expense.

You must pay the full cost of the premium plus 2 percent (102 percent is the maximum you can be charged), but the cost will be far less than what you would spend for an individual insurance plan. The COBRA provisions apply to those who are terminated from employment, change their status from full-time to part-time, spouses and families of an employee who dies or becomes eligible for Medicare, spouses who are divorced from an employee who is covered by a group plan, and older children who exceed the age maximum of the employer's plan. In 1989, Congress expanded COBRA coverage for those who are disabled at "the qualifying event" (either termination of employment or reduction in hours). People in that situation can continue with COBRA for twenty-nine months, rather than eighteen, although they may be charged up to 150 percent of the applicable premium for months nineteen through twenty-nine. This extension offers important protection to the disabled, since there is a five-month waiting period for Social Security disability cash benefits, and an additional two-year waiting period for Medicare benefits.

Once you are no longer able to continue with your group coverage under COBRA, you will be eligible to sign up for coverage under a conversion plan. The coverage provided by these plans is usually skimpy and the premiums very high. In general, only people with serious medical problems that require extensive care find that it pays to subscribe to a conversion plan.

Coverage for Older Children

COBRA requires that group insurance be extended to older children in their late teens and early twenties, depending on the maximum age for the employer's plan. For older children with a disease such as diabetes or cancer that makes them uninsurable, the group insurance you can obtain through COBRA would be the best temporary solution. For healthy older children, however, the premium rates are apt to be extremely high, and you might be able to find a less expensive alternative.

Most colleges and universities offer student health insurance, often for premiums as low as $200 a year. Coverage is not very comprehensive, but if the plan provides protection for serious problems and has an affordable maximum out-of-pocket expense, college-sponsored insurance may be a worthwhile alternative to covering your children through your employer's group plan or under your individual family policy.

Age-Rated Indemnity Policies

Most, if not all, states allow insurance companies to set premiums based on actuarial projections of health care costs for people in a given age group. This practice is called "age-rating," and it favors younger people. Because teenagers and young adults belong to an age group that uses comparatively few health services, they may be able to find an age-rated plan with a very reasonable premium—perhaps as low as $40 a month.

If You Are Turned Down for Insurance

In some cases if you have a preexisting condition, you may be faced with purchasing a health care plan that excludes the condition either for an unacceptable waiting period or perhaps permanently, or you may not be able to find a plan that will accept you at all, even though you may no longer be affected by the condition. If you are rejected for coverage, contact the Disclosure Office of the Medical Information Bureau (P.O. Box 801, Boston, Massachusetts 02103; Tel: 617/329-4500). Some insurance companies, rather than doing their own evaluation, check an applicant's health status with this organization. When you call or write, you may learn of misinformation in your medical history that is the cause of the rejection.

Many states are now developing programs for people who can afford insurance but who have a preexisting condition that prevents them from obtaining coverage or causes insurers to offer coverage at an exorbitant premium rate. These "risk pool" programs offer coverage that in many ways is similar to major medical policies. Most feature a deductible and co-insurance payments, a stop-loss on out-of-pocket expenses (generally higher than major medical plans), and a lifetime maximum on insurer payments (generally lower than major medical plans). While preexisting conditions will be covered eventually, most programs impose a waiting period.

Premium rates in high-risk pools are determined by formulas that vary from state to state. In Minnesota, for example, the state-sponsored risk-pool premium is calculated as 125 percent of the commercial premium rate for comparable coverage. In Montana, at the other extreme, the formula is 400 percent of the commercial premium rate. Most of the other states operating risk pools set premium rates within the lower end of this range.

Your eligibility for coverage by a risk pool is generally determined by your either having been rejected by one (or in some states two) commercial carriers or by having been offered insurance by a commercial carrier (or in some states two carriers) at a higher premium rate than that of the pool. You will be considered as having been rejected if the coverage that is offered to you places a waiver or exclusion on your preexisting condition.

Some states' risk pool programs offer Medigap coverage, which is important for people under 65 who are receiving

Medicare disability benefits but who, because of their age, are not eligible for conventional Medigap coverage.

As of early summer, 1990, the following states are operating risk pool programs or will be soon: California (not yet operating), Connecticut, Florida, Georgia (not yet operating), Illinois, Indiana, Iowa, Maine, Minnesota, Montana, Nebraska, New Mexico, North Dakota, Oregon, South Carolina, Tennessee, Texas (not yet operating), Washington, and Wisconsin. Utah and Wyoming have passed legislation to establish risk pools, as well.

If You Cannot Afford Insurance

Both federal and state governments are beginning to pay more attention to the so-called medically indigent, primarily employed people who make too much money to qualify for Medicaid and too little to be able to afford any health insurance plan. Hawaii has required employers to provide some insurance to all workers for a number of years. Massachusetts passed a law in 1988 requiring employers to offer insurance to their employees or pay a tax to fund an insurance program for them. Oregon gives small employers a tax credit if they agree to provide health insurance. Washington State has created a pilot program to extend health insurance to the medically indigent by charging them premiums on a sliding scale and offering medical care through a choice of managed health care systems. At the national level, there is increasing interest in exploring some form of universal health insurance. It is not likely that the United States will enter the twenty-first century without a major federal program to deal with the problem of the uninsured.

Protection for People with Indemnity Insurance

Indemnity insurance is usually designed to reimburse you for medical bills *after* they have been generated. Thus, your indemnity carrier does not concern itself with the *quality* of care you receive, nor will it direct you to high-quality physicians or hospitals or monitor your ongoing medical care. One exception to this general rule is found in policies that require you to seek the opinion of more than one doctor before you will be reimbursed for certain procedures. Insurance companies have saved considerable amounts of money with these programs, and policyholders have been spared much unnecessary surgery.

By excluding coverage for care provided by nonlicensed practitioners and by refusing reimbursement for procedures with no proven medical value, indemnity insurance plans may indirectly protect you from your own poor judgment or the poor judgment of your physician. But it's up to you to know *before* you receive treatment that a practitioner does not have the proper credentials or that the care that is being recommended will not be reimbursed. Otherwise, you may receive worthless—or worse—treatment and have to pay for it out of pocket.

For the most part, commercial indemnity insurers and the Blues put their efforts into protecting themselves from fraudulent bills or from excess charges. Medicare and Medicaid monitor billings, looking both for fraud (there has been an 800% increase since 1981 in health-fraud-related felony convictions) and for physicians who order a suspicious number of tests, procedures, and drugs.

If you choose indemnity insurance coverage, you will need to rely on your own efforts to assure yourself of quality medical care. There is very little regulation of independent physicians, doctors are reluctant to censure their peers, and county and state medical societies are slow to take action against incompetent or impaired physicians. Many patients may be injured before an unfit doctor finally loses his or her license.

Fee-for-service physicians in solo practice or small groups do not have effective systems for monitoring their outpatient practices. At present, the best quality assurance measures in fee-for-service medicine are usually found in larger high-quality medical groups that carefully screen new physicians and monitor their ongoing medical practice. That such efforts are necessary was verified by a study reported in *The New England Journal of Medicine*, which found that 5 percent of physicians applying for clinical positions at ambulatory care clinics had false credentials in their applications.[3]

If you are a patient in a hospital, your physician will receive closer scrutiny. Quality-of-care committees monitor the hospital care provided by physicians, and they can suspend hospital admitting privileges if they find incompetence.

Does Indemnity Insurance Suit Your Nonfinancial Needs?

We have focused mainly on the financial aspects of indemnity insurance. But there are other considerations that may lead you to choose or reject it. You will have to fill out claim forms and keep orderly, detailed records of your medical expenses and reimbursements to use indemnity insurance efficiently. You must meet deadlines in order for your claim to be considered legitimate. You may also have to discuss fees with your physicians, something not everyone is comfortable doing.

On the other hand, you may not mind the paperwork, and you may want the freedom of choice of providers and hospitals that indemnity insurance offers. Perhaps you have a trusted personal physician whose name does not appear on the roster of a PPO or HMO you are offered. Continuity of care is an important feature of good medical care, and indemnity insurance may be the only choice that allows you to continue a valued medical relationship.

2

Health Maintenance Organizations: Where They Came from and How They Work

A Health Maintenance Organization (HMO) is a prepaid medical plan that offers both coverage for medical care *and* the care itself. When you join one, either as an individual member or through your company, you or your employer pays a monthly sum to the plan you've chosen. The HMO then assumes responsibility for your medical expenses as long as you use the providers and services it designates.

HMOs may be tightly managed group practice plans or loosely organized associations of physicians practicing in their own offices. They may be independent organizations or they may be sponsored by commercial insurance companies like CIGNA or Prudential, by Blue Cross, by hospitals, by physicians' associations, or by unions, employers, or consumers.

Nationally, HMOs enroll close to 20 percent of employees who have group health plans, and they are currently offered to more than 50 percent of the work force that receives health insurance from employers. Yet, despite the widespread availability of HMOs, many people remain confused about how they operate and the quality of care they provide.

The Genesis and Growth of the HMO Movement

Until the 1970s, prepaid medical plans were available in only a few specific locations, including Minneapolis, Seattle, Los Angeles, Boston, and Washington, D.C. Since then, HMO membership in these cities has grown substantially, in some cases eclipsing all other forms of health insurance. By 1989, in Seattle, 560,000 people had signed up with nine HMOs; in Minneapolis, 750,000 had joined seven HMOs. Sixty-five percent of the total population, or 400,000 people, now belong to three HMOs in the District of Columbia. In Massachusetts, 25.1 percent of the population receive care in HMOs, with 1.1 million people concentrated in ten HMOs in the Boston area.

Overall, 30 percent of the population of California belong to HMOs. In greater Los Angeles, more than four million people have signed up with seventeen HMOs; in the Bay Area, 2.7 million belong to eleven HMOs.

In other regions, where HMOs took root at a somewhat later date, membership figures are still significant. In Ohio, for example, there are now 1.4 million members of thirty-five HMOs. As of January 1, 1990, 34 million Americans were enrolled in 575 plans.[1]

These numbers reflect an important trend and a threat to the customary fee-for-service style of practice of American physicians. Rather than being paid by the patient and/or insurance carrier for each service rendered, HMO physicians are allotted a monthly sum to cover medical care for a specified number of patients. This change in reimbursement makes physicians far more accountable for the medical resources they use, and it has led to controversy within the medical profession.

"The history of medicine has been written as an epic of progress," observes Paul Starr, a Princeton-based social historian, "but it is also a tale of social and economic conflict over the emergence of new hierarchies of power and authority, new markets, and new conditions of belief and experience."[2] In our century, we have seen physicians first oppose, and then endorse, indemnity health insurance, and they are following the same pattern of resisting, and then accepting, prepaid health plans. This pattern of initial resistance has emotional and economic roots that cannot be ignored, and a quick look at the past sheds light on the present-day controversy.

HMOs as Social Experiments

The era that gave birth to indemnity health insurance also hatched the first prepaid health plans. For their first two or three decades, prepaid plans were privately financed social experiments designed to provide medical care and insurance to working people. Some were organized by physicians and others by consumer groups. In the late 1920s and 1930s in California, the Ross-Loos Clinic and the Kaiser-Permanente plan sprang into existence as practical efforts to finance health care for blue-collar workers. During the 1940s, a group of consumers named themselves Group Health Cooperative of Puget Sound and pooled their resources to buy medical care at an affordable price. These plans were all prepaid group practices. Consumers who signed up received all their health care from a group of physicians who were paid either a salary or a per capita amount rather than a fee for each visit or procedure.

Advocates of similar projects that were undertaken in other parts of the country in the 1950s and 1960s shared a similar view: prepayment was a way to make medical care accessible and affordable to people who might otherwise have to go without it. During this period, prepaid plans were bitterly opposed by the American Medical Association (AMA), which labeled as "unethical" any attempt on the part of nonphysicians to control physicians' fees or working conditions.

Most AMA members considered these plans a threat to their style of practice.[3] When new ones opened, those physicians who agreed to participate in them were often censured by local medical societies, labeled as "communists" or "socialists" by their colleagues, denied hospital privileges, and in many places threatened with the loss of their license to practice.

In 1929, for example, the physicians of Elk City, Oklahoma, rose up in opposition to the brainchild of a man they had formerly regarded as their esteemed colleague, a well-to-do doctor named Michael Shadid. Concerned about the difficulty many farmers faced when it came to paying their medical bills, Shadid proposed to his fellow physicians that they join together to establish a health plan using the agricultural cooperative as a model. Members would subscribe $50 to build a hospital and hire physicians and would then receive health care at a discounted rate from the Farmers' Union Cooperative Hospital Association, as the plan came to be called.

While a few local physicians were interested in the idea, most were outraged. They invoked the AMA "unethical" label, sought to have Shadid's license revoked, dissolved the local medical society and then reinstituted it without him as a member, undertook court actions against him, and attempted to change state laws so that the new plan could be declared illegal. Despite efforts to destroy it over a span of twenty years, the plan grew and became a model for other plans; eventually its physicians even served as leaders in the local medical society.

This same pattern occurred repeatedly: initial opposition by the medical profession was followed by growing acceptance as physicians began to work with prepaid plans. Over the years, the opposition of organized medicine subsided, and by 1959 a committee of the AMA found no legitimate basis for opposing group health plans.[4]

During the 1960s, health planners began to promote the expansion of prepaid plans not only as a way of making care affordable but also as a method for saving money by discouraging wasteful practices. Enthusiasts believed that these plans presented improvements in both the quality of insurance coverage and the quality of medical care. Consumer groups, hospitals, universities, and not-for-profit organizations became interested in prepaid medicine, and by the early 1970s a number of plans had been established, including Group Health Incorporated of Minneapolis-St. Paul (initiated and run by consumers), the Harvard Community Health Plan (started by Harvard University), and the ANCHOR Plan for Health Maintenance (established by Rush-Presbyterian-St. Luke's Medical Center in Chicago). During this time, Blue Cross began to organize and offer prepaid plans as alternatives to its indemnity policies.

The Federal Government Steps In

In 1970, with political pressure building to create a federal health insurance program, the Nixon administration embraced prepaid medicine as a way to control costs, offer comprehensive coverage, and keep health care firmly planted in the private sector. The prepaid plan, once labeled "socialistic" or "communistic," was now renamed "health maintenance organization" and was proposed by the conservative Nixon administration as a free-market alternative to the far more radical prospect of a national health insurance program.

The HMO Act of 1973 provided start-up grants and loans as a way to stimulate the creation of plans. The Act also allowed plans that had received government approval to operate in those states with laws barring limitation of freedom of choice for patients, and it required employers with more than twenty-five employees to offer membership in government-approved HMOs as an alternative to indemnity insurance. The debate over prepaid medicine sprang up with new vigor, with physicians committed to fee-for-service practice arguing that the government loans created unfair competition and some employers complaining of government interference. The grant and loan program was discontinued by the Reagan administration in 1982, leaving behind the Office of Prepaid Health Care (OPHC), an agency that continues to monitor federally approved HMOs.

The Advent of Independent Practice Associations (IPAs)

In the late 1950s, physicians in California's San Joaquin Valley, concerned by the rapid growth that the Kaiser-Permanente plan was experiencing in the area, decided to offer their own prepaid plans. A number of county medical societies launched organizations called Medical Care Foundations, which provided health care benefits similar to those offered by Kaiser but delivered care in the offices of fee-for-service physicians.

As physicians in other areas faced increasing competition from the rapid growth of HMOs, the idea spread, and a number of these more loosely structured organizations were created. The insurance arm, or HMO, would enroll members and handle claims, but the physicians would continue to practice in their own offices, caring for both fee-for-service patients and HMO members. When the HMO Act was passed, provision was made for this type of organization, which is now called an Independent (or Individual) Practice Association (IPA).

Doctors garnered marketing advantages from this approach. Where group practice HMOs limited the numbers of physicians who could participate, IPAs opened the doors. Many of these plans welcomed all physicians who wished to join—an IPA might list five hundred to one thousand doctors on its roster. In order to be part of the plan, doctors agreed to give discounts on their usual fees to the IPA. They also allowed the plan to withhold an additional percentage of their fees and place it in an escrow fund to pay for unexpected expenses. At the end of the year, money that remained in the fund would be given to the physicians as a bonus.

Enter Wall Street

By the late 1970s, as HMOs continued to grow, commercial insurers like Prudential, John Hancock, and the company now known as CIGNA, anxious to protect their share of the health insurance market, began to organize prepaid medical plans. At the same time, the financial world suddenly envisioned prepaid medicine as a potential gold mine, and for-profit hospital chains, venture capitalists, and investors rushed in to stake their claims.

Some of these new players bought established group practice plans or founded new ones, but making money in group practice HMOs took time. Established plans were sold only when they were in financial trouble and in need of an infusion of capital, and new plans required a sizable investment in staff and facilities. Unlike most of the earlier creators of prepaid group practice plans, who established their plans to fulfill social goals, the founders of these new ventures expected a handsome profit for their efforts.

The Lure of IPAs

IPAs promised the rapid growth and profitability that a group practice plan could not deliver. They were far less costly and time-consuming to initiate. All that was necessary was a small administrative staff and a drawerful of contracts with physicians and hospitals—or so it seemed. To increase their appeal to additional investors, they could be designed to grow quickly, and grow they did. New national organizations with names like AmeriCare, HealthAmerica, HMO America, and Maxicare sprang up, signed contracts with thousands of physicians around the country, and embarked on aggressive, expensive—and successful—marketing campaigns for new members.

Hidden in the advantages that attracted investors, physicians, and members were serious traps. All those members brought in revenues, but they also piled up medical bills. All those doctors who signed contracts with the plan used medical resources, and the administrators of these new decentralized plans did not have the management skills to control utilization of resources or to influence physicians to use resources in a more cost-conscious manner.

The "doom loop." As medical costs spiraled upward, a plan would be forced to increase its premiums, and the composition of its subscribers would begin to change. IPAs that had formerly enrolled a representative cross-section of patients began to attract people who were willing to pay higher rates only because they knew they would need the comprehensive benefits the plan offered. Thus, a plan that was already in financial trouble might attract an ever sicker and more expensive population.

Participating physicians were often surprised and angry when they found there was no money in the contingency fund for the year-end bonuses they had been led to expect. As the now precarious plans asked providers for bigger and bigger discounts, doctors fled. Eventually, swamped by medical bills, many of the ambitious new plans ran out of funds, and news of their failure dismayed members and investors alike.

During this period some IPAs managed to survive and prosper. Two national networks that did—U.S. Healthcare and United HealthCare—between them now enroll over two million members. Most of those IPAs that survived did so by changing the ways in which they selected, paid, and monitored physicians, and by controlling access to medical services.

Controlling access. Members who referred themselves to expensive specialists for problems that could be treated by generalists had the potential to escalate costs considerably. The solution to this problem lay in the introduction of the "gatekeeper," or "care-manager," approach. Each member would be required to identify one of the plan's primary care physicians as his or her family doctor. This physician would then be responsible for authorizing referrals to specialists and other medical services. Well-managed IPAs that use this approach have been successful, although their premiums are usually somewhat higher than the more tightly managed group practice plans they compete with.

The End of the HMO Honeymoon

For many years, prepaid plans enjoyed a kind of financial honeymoon. A properly managed plan had no difficulty attracting employers eager to save on health care expenses, and its careful use of hospital services alone could keep premium increases well below those charged by its indemnity-based competitors. But when government programs and indemnity insurers began to cut costs with their own measures, HMOs lost their easy competitive edge and were compelled to work much harder to expand their share of the market.

In 1988 and 1989, indemnity premium rates soared, some by as much as 40 to 60 percent, whereas increases in HMO premiums ranged from 15 to 25 percent. In 1987–88, the average increase in premiums for prepaid plans was 16.8 percent for singles and 16.6 percent for families, in contrast to average increases of more than 20 percent for indemnity insurance.

Meanwhile, as the HMO movement grew, competition between prepaid plans increased as well. HMOs had been designed to compete with traditional indemnity plans, not with one another, and the intensely competitive years of 1987, 1988, and 1989 saw a slowing of the dramatic growth they had enjoyed in the mid-1980s. Toward the end of the 1980s, publicly traded HMO stocks dropped in price, and commercial insurance companies lost large sums on their prepaid plans. In fact, in 1987 and 1988 two-thirds of HMOs lost money, resulting in a number of mergers and consolidations.

This upheaval in the HMO industry has made some consumers apprehensive about joining. The dust is still settling as companies leave the HMO field and larger organizations absorb unsuccessful competitors.

The Current Climate

Throughout their development, HMOs have challenged or disappointed various groups. Fee-for-service physicians interested in retaining control over fee-setting realized that they would either have to compete with HMOs or else work for them at a substantial discount or for a salary. Employers, accustomed to having a free hand in deciding what insurance to offer, disliked the fact that they could be required by law to offer HMO membership in addition to the regular company plan. Investors, lured initially by the prospect of easy money, were disappointed by the uncertainties of operating an HMO and by the length of time it took to develop a solidly profitable plan.

During the long struggle to establish prepaid medicine as a legitimate alternative to fee-for-service practice, doctors defending the medical status quo have raised essentially the same concerns they did when indemnity health insurance was first proposed. They argue that the sanctity of the relationship between patient-payer and physician-payee is endangered by admitting the HMO as a third party. The HMO, they contend, might be willing to sacrifice the well-being of the individual patient in order to save or to make money, and thus the quality of medical care will suffer.

Physicians who advocate prepaid medicine, on the other hand, argue that it allows doctors to deliver quality care that the average person can afford. The late William MacColl, a founding physician of Group Health Cooperative of Puget Sound, spoke for this position when he maintained that "If one accepts the proposition that in our economy of abundance good health is a basic right, then to put it up for sale on a piece work basis on the seller's terms would appear to be inconsistent."[5]

Charges and countercharges will no doubt continue to fly, but critics of prepaid medicine have been urged by Arnold S. Relman, M.D., editor of *The New England Journal of Medicine*, to be "more receptive to experiments like HMOs and primary care networks. All too often in the past, established professional groups have resisted such experiments, leading to the public impression that they were sometimes more concerned about their own economic interests than the public welfare."[6]

What were once seen as clinics designed for farmers and laborers now appeal to diverse groups of customers—white-collar and blue-collar workers, professionals, and people in Medicaid and Medicare programs. Prepaid practice is now an established alternative to traditional fee-for-service medicine.

Why Doctors Choose to Work in HMOs

Most people are familiar with the reasons doctors choose fee-for-service practice—independence, ownership, freedom from interference—and they understand why most doctors sign up with an IPA—the ability to attract new patients and retain those who prefer prepaid coverage but want continuity in their doctor-patient relationship. But many people want to know why good doctors, who might have opened their own practices, would choose instead to work for a group practice HMO.

Working in a prepaid group removes some of the financial pressures that exist in a fee-for-service group practice while providing a working environment that facilitates doctors' sharing their knowledge with colleagues. Moreover, it relieves doctors of the burdens of running a small business, which they must shoulder in a fee-for-service practice.

Prepaid practice appeals to many doctors because it allows them to deliver comprehensive and coordinated care without worrying about whether or not the patient can afford to pay for a particular test or treatment. Health care centers equipped with lab and X-ray facilities on the premises give doctors quick access to the diagnostic information they need. Depending on the size of the health care center they work in, physicians may be able to send patients to an on-site pharmacy or to resident physical therapists, nutrition counselors, and mental health professionals. Only the largest fee-for-service group practices contain such extensive resources for physicians and their patients.

Some candidates apply for HMO jobs because they like the style of practice. Primary care physicians play an important role as care managers in HMOs and therefore are able to stay involved with their patients. Specialists spend 100 percent of their time and effort in their own areas of expertise. They can rely on the primary care physicians to refer only those patients who need specialty care.

Physicians who join a group practice HMO can count on dependable incomes and substantial fringe benefits. Most plans pay for continuing medical education, malpractice insurance, sick leave, vacations, and retirement benefits; some even offer paid sabbaticals. Total compensation for salaried primary care physicians is competitive with fee-for-service practice in most parts of the country. In addition, physicians who want more time with their families may choose prepaid practice because they will work fewer hours and have lighter call schedules than doctors in fee-for-service practice, who often work an eighty-hour week and spend many nights on call.

Some physicians see HMO practice as a stepping-stone to developing their own fee-for-service practice. A young doctor may decide to work for an HMO for a few years in order to pay off medical school debts and establish a presence in the community. Once these goals are accomplished, he or she may leave to open an office.

Overall, physicians in group practice HMOs are happy with their choice. A poll taken by Louis Harris and Associates showed that all physicians, whatever their type of practice, expressed comparable levels of satisfaction with their work. Physicians in HMOs expressed particular satisfaction with three aspects of their system: professional peer support, affiliation with a major medical center, and time for family, friends, and nonprofessional interests.[7]

Different Types of HMOs

There are a number of ways in which HMOs can be organized. Following is a summary of the basic characteristics of different types of plans.

Group Practice HMOs

To most people, the term "HMO" means a group practice plan with its own health care centers and physicians. From a prospective member's point of view, all group practice plans look pretty much the same, but there are differences in the way they are organized. Some are *staff* models in which the physicians are employees of the HMO itself. Thus, a single organization is responsible for selling health care coverage, processing claims, and hiring and monitoring physicians. Others are *group* models: a physicians' group forms a partnership that contracts with the HMO (the administrative entity) to provide medical services to HMO members. Often, group model HMOs have been developed by an established fee-for-service medical group.

Group practice plans of both types have their own outpatient medical facilities, which offer a number of services in centralized locations. A typical health care center in one of these plans provides physician, laboratory, and X-ray services, and often additional services such as pharmacy, vision care, and mental health treatment. Sizes of health care centers vary. Some plans have one large multispecialty center with dozens of physicians; others supplement their large centers with smaller satellite centers. Very large plans may own hospitals. In general, group practice plans offer extensive health education services, and many have long lists of classes and support groups from which to choose. As of January 1990, there were 124 group practice plans in operation, caring for 13.5 million members.

Independent Practice Associations (IPA-model HMOs)

IPA-model HMOs contain two parts: an administrative arm, which develops and markets the benefits package, handles claims-processing, contracts with physicians, and monitors their performance; and the health delivery arm, which consists of fee-for-service physicians. These physicians, working in their own offices, see HMO members along with their regular patients.

In addition to plans created by insurance companies and investors, many IPAs have been organized by hospitals and medical societies; their affiliated physicians form an association—the IPA. That association then represents the physicians in contracting with the insurance arm—the HMO. Physicians who work with IPAs either give the HMO a discount on their regular fees or accept "capitation." Capitation is a fee paid by the plan to its doctors for each plan member they agree to care for, no matter how many visits that member needs in a given year. These fees are renegotiated annually by the HMO administration and its participating physicians.

You may encounter variations on the IPA theme, with names like "network model HMOs" and "primary care networks." Network model HMOs contract with individual medical *groups*, which agree to provide services to HMO members in addition to their regular fee-for-service practice. Primary care networks contract either with individual primary care providers (family practitioners, pediatricians, general internists) or with primary care groups. These primary care givers are then responsible for all referrals for other medical care. As of January 1990 there were 362 IPAs in operation, caring for 13.8 million members, and eighty-nine network plans, caring for 5.8 million members.

Mixed Models, or Hybrid HMOs

As competition for premium dollars continues to escalate, some HMOs have begun to create programs that provide several options: group practice plans, IPAs, networks, and even PPOs. For example, the Rush-Presbyterian-St. Luke's Medical Center in Chicago runs a group practice plan, an IPA, and a PPO—as does the CIGNA Healthplan in Los Angeles.

Point-of-Service Plans

The newest wrinkle in the health insurance business is a plan, often organized by an HMO, that offers members a choice between HMO coverage and indemnity coverage each time they need medical care. They can use prepaid providers and receive full coverage or choose nonparticipating physicians instead and receive partial coverage. The financial penalties are generally severe for using providers outside the plan. You may have to pay 25 to 30 percent of charges after meeting a deductible of $200 to $250. Eighty-four HMOs now offer "open-ended" or "point-of-service" plans to employers, and as of January 1990, 750,000 people were members of this kind of plan.

The Business Side of HMOs

By comparison with indemnity plans charging comparable premiums, HMOs supply more coverage and require members to share less of the cost of care. They are usually less expensive than the handful of remaining "Cadillac" indemnity plans that offer extensive benefits, 90 to 100 percent coverage, and low deductibles. How do HMOs do it? By controlling the *delivery* as well as the financing of health care. In contrast to indemnity insurance, which pays for care after it is given, HMOs are able to choose and utilize health care resources that match the needs of their members.

Hospitals

HMOs look for high-quality, well-run hospitals and negotiate favorable rates with them. A few very large HMOs like Kaiser-Permanente and Group Health Cooperative of Puget Sound run their own hospitals in areas where they have particularly high concentrations of subscribers.

Physicians

HMOs try to hire, or contract with, the most cost-effective physicians in their communities. Practice styles vary dramatically from physician to physician. Some order more expensive tests and perform far more procedures than others, yet there is little or no correlation between the quality of care physicians provide and the costs they generate. Indemnity plans must pay for the services rendered by any physician a patient chooses, regardless of that physician's practice style.

Discounts

When HMOs make contracts with physicians and hospitals, they can negotiate substantial discounts because they can guarantee a large volume of patients.

Utilization Management

HMOs have utilization management programs to ensure that members do not receive unnecessary medical care. Special committees review charts of patients with unusually long and costly hospitalizations to determine whether there are other more effective treatments or less expensive, less invasive treatments that might be equally effective.

Resources

Group practice models have built-in efficiencies. They can hire the right number of physicians in the right mix of specialties for their membership. They can plan for facilities in locations and sizes that best accommodate the needs of their members, and they can provide those facilities with equipment to do a number of procedures on site. Those plans that own hospitals need only maintain the number of beds their membership requires, an economy that enables them to keep their hospitals full.

Lower Administrative Costs

HMOs require far less paperwork to run than do indemnity insurers (including Medicare and Medicaid). A national study of health care costs found that overall, 22 percent of total health care expenditures are eaten up by administrative costs. In 1989 HMOs averaged 12.8 percent in administrative costs.[8]

HMO Coverage

HMOs offer more comprehensive insurance coverage than do indemnity plans. Federally qualified HMOs must cover preexisting conditions (PECs), and most other HMOs also cover them. Waiting periods are seldom required before coverage begins, and coverage for most care, both in and out of the hospital, is usually more extensive than that of an indemnity plan.

Virtually all of the HMOs that responded to a survey conducted in 1989 by the Group Health Association of America (GHAA) fully cover inpatient care for medical and surgical problems, primary care visits, outpatient laboratory and outpatient radiology, prenatal care, emergency care, home health care, skilled nursing care, drug and alcohol detoxification, physical therapy, allergy treatment, and inhalation therapy. In addition, more than 90 percent of plans cover hearing, vision, and speech tests and pharmacy services. More than 75 percent of the plans surveyed have benefits for hospice care, podiatry services, dental services for accidental injuries, durable medical equipment, external prosthetics, occupational therapy, and drug and alcohol rehabilitation.

One hundred percent of plans surveyed cover outpatient mental health services, and 91 percent covered inpatient mental health treatment, but usually with limits and copayments. Commonly, members are entitled to twenty outpatient visits and thirty days of mental health treatment in a hospital per year. Seventy-nine percent of plans with coverage for mental health services require a co-payment for outpatient treatment, with the average charge being $16 a visit.

Eighty-six percent of plans covered hospitalization in full. Some plans, however, require co-payments of, for example, $100 a day for the first five days. Almost all plans cover kidney, corneal, and bone-marrow transplants as well as liver transplants for children with biliary atresia or a related condition. Heart transplants are covered by 72 percent of the

HMOs surveyed. Liver transplants for adults are covered by almost 63 percent of plans.

Coverage for Preventive Services

Almost all the HMOs surveyed offer full coverage for well-baby care, pap tests, mammography, influenza shots, childhood and adult immunizations, and routine physicals. Nutrition counseling is covered by 85 percent of the HMOs, and health education classes are covered by 75 percent of the plans.

Prescription Drug Benefits

Of the 94 percent of plans that cover prescription drugs, almost all do so with no limitations on how many prescriptions members may fill, although single purchases may be limited to one month's supply. Eighty-five percent of plans have no pharmacy deductible; of those that do, most call for $50 a year.[9]

Special Programs and Services

Most HMOs cover eye exams for children and adults, but other optical services vary. Group practice plans often run their own optical shops, and some plans may offer free prescription lenses, savings on the purchase of frames and contact lenses, and free or low-cost repairs.

Many HMOs offer health education classes and support groups at little or no cost to members. Exercise, weight reduction, and stop-smoking classes sponsored by HMOs may be a real bargain over independent programs. Some group practice plans offer choices of programs ranging from prenatal fitness classes to ski conditioning to meal planning for diabetics.

Limitations on Services

Following are services that HMOs commonly do *not* pay for or will pay for within specified limits and/or restrictions:

- *Mental health benefits:* Usually limited to short-term treatment (a twenty-visit maximum is common)
- *Physical therapy:* Often restricted to treatment of problems for which significant improvement is anticipated within a two-month period
- *Abortion:* May not be a covered benefit; in such cases, some plans provide the service and bill the member
- *Controversial surgery:* HMOs usually exclude such procedures as gastric stapling, temporo-mandibular joint (TMJ) surgery, radial keratotomy, and preventive subcutaneous mastectomy, none of which has been established as medically effective.
- *Nontraditional health care:* Like most indemnity companies, most HMOs provide minimal or no coverage for care provided by nontraditional practitioners such as naturopaths, homeopaths, iridologists, reflexologists, and unlicensed mental health practitioners. Chiropractic treatment may be covered if so mandated by state law. You should check with the office of your state insurance commissioner to determine whether chiropractic or any other nontraditional forms of care have been mandated for coverage where you live. Even in states that mandate coverage for chiropractic care, you must usually be referred to the chiropractor by the HMO.

How HMO Insurance Differs from Indemnity

Whereas indemnity insurance pays for your care *after* you have selected and received it, HMOs give you coverage and health care in one integrated system. You must receive your medical care from hospitals, physicians, and other providers of medical services designated or approved by the HMO, with the exception of emergency care, or urgent care you need when you are traveling away from the HMO's service area.

Benefits

Most indemnity plans do not reimburse you for the kinds of preventive services covered by HMOs. For families with young children or people who regularly use preventive services, HMOs offer a clear advantage. HMOs are also much more apt to cover the cost of vision care, allergy treatment, hearing tests, prescription drugs, home health care, and a number of other services than are indemnity plans.

Payments

HMOs charge a monthly premium; however, there are rarely deductibles or a co-insurance percentage to pay. Indemnity plans shift costs by having you pay co-insurance—that is, you pay a percentage of the fee for a given service covered by the plan, commonly 20 percent (after satisfying the initial deductible.) If, for example, your visit to the doctor costs $100, you would pay $20 and your insurance would pick up $80, once the deductible is satisfied.

Most HMOs now shift costs as well, but in a far more limited way. As an HMO member, you will probably pay a nominal sum, which is called a "co-payment," each time you utilize the services of the plan. For example, an office visit might require a co-payment of $3 to $5. The exact amount will depend on the terms of the plan your employer provides. A typical plan (sometimes referred to as a 3/3/25 plan in the HMO business) would require a co-payment of $3 for an office visit, $3 for a prescription, and $25 for a visit to a hospital emergency room. Some plans also have a co-payment for hospitalization—perhaps $100 per admission, or $100 per day for up to five days.

Like indemnity insurance plans, almost all HMOS have a ceiling (stop-loss) on co-payments that limits the total amount you would have to pay in one year. Federally qualified HMOs use an intricate formula that sets an annual per-person limit on co-payments at approximately $2,000. Plans that are not federally qualified are apt to have a similar ceiling, commonly $750–$1,000 per year for an individual and twice that for a family.

Whereas the presence and level of stop-loss is one of the most important features of an indemnity plan, it is much less important in an HMO, which puts its members at much less financial risk. An average healthy person or even an average unhealthy person would be unlikely to reach the ceiling specified in a typical HMO plan. For example, a family of four who made fifteen office visits a year at $5 a visit and filled ten prescriptions at $3 each, would spend $105 on co-payments for those office visits and prescriptions. A person with a chronic disease who required twenty physician visits a year and two prescriptions a month at the same co-payment rates would spend $172.

On the other hand, someone who suffered from several chronic diseases, took a number of medications on a regular basis, made frequent office visits, required such special services as physical therapy, went to the emergency room several times a year, and entered the hospital once or twice a year might well reach the stop-loss limit, especially if large co-payments were required for hospitalization. In this situation, a stop-loss on co-payments would offer meaningful protection.

How HMOs Manage Your Care

Restricted choice of physicians and hospitals. All care must be arranged for or provided by physicians and hospitals associated with the plan. Typically, members are asked to select a family doctor from a list of primary care physicians; that doctor is then responsible for managing their care and referring them to specialists as necessary.

In most HMOs, members must be referred to specialists by their primary care physician. Depending on the size of the HMO and the specialty, the HMO may have several of its own staff specialists or may contract with specialists in the community. HMOs generally cover the cost of second opinions but will usually limit the choice of physicians available for consultation. In addition, members are required to use hospitals specified by the HMO.

Prior authorization. Members who receive medical care without HMO approval must pay for that care out of their own pockets, with two exceptions: true emergencies, such as choking, crushing chest pain, uncontrollable bleeding, and serious fractures; and urgent problems while traveling away from the HMO's service area. In these situations, you must usually notify the HMO within a specified period of time that you have received medical attention, and the HMO will reimburse you for the costs of the care it determines was medically necessary. The price for failing to notify the HMO may be no coverage at all.

Although some indemnity and PPO plans have notification requirements, the price of ignoring them is generally less steep; policyholders may end up with less coverage rather than none. For example, a PPO member who does not use a preferred provider will commonly be required to pay 20–30 percent of the costs of the care, not 100 percent. Someone covered by an indemnity plan who fails to check with the insurance company might have to pay 50 percent of the cost of a hospitalization if the plan requires that the procedure be performed in an outpatient setting.

An approved list of medications (formulary). A fee-for-service physician can prescribe any medication that has been approved by the FDA. HMO pharmacies dispense only those FDA-approved drugs that have been accepted by a committee composed of HMO pharmacists and physicians who review drugs for safety, efficacy, and cost-effectiveness. HMOs often use generic drugs when they are as effective as those that carry brand names. Physicians who want to prescribe a drug that is not dispensed by the HMO pharmacy can do so, but they must be able to justify its use in order for their patient to receive the HMO's usual coverage for drugs. New or unusually expensive drugs may not be covered unless the HMO's formulary committee has determined that they are safer or more effective than an established drug—or unless there is no other drug that will treat a given condition.

Integration of care and coverage. The claims forms typical of indemnity policies are unnecessary in HMOs because care and coverage are provided by the same organization. Any covered benefit recommended by an HMO doctor will be paid for by the plan. In this type of system, physicians may be able to make medical arrangements for their patients that they could not provide under the rules of indemnity insurance. Many HMOs, for example, will train parents of a newborn with jaundice to use the special lights that treat this condition, so that they can take their baby home from the hospital. The HMO provides the lighting equipment, and the baby is tested each day to make sure the treatment is progressing properly. The HMO's motivation to reduce medical expenses, especially hospital costs, may work to the advantage of those patients who want greater involvement in their care or who would like to stay out of the hospital if possible, or shorten hospital stays once they are no longer acutely ill.

How HMOs Ensure Quality

A good HMO emphasizes staff recruitment and, like a highly selective college, a plan with a strong reputation for quality medical care will have more applicants than one with lower standards. In a high-quality HMO, more than 90 percent of physicians will be board-certified or board-eligible. How an HMO selects physicians and examines their credentials depends to some extent on the type of plan.

Group practice plans. Good group practice HMOs, like good fee-for-service groups, have fairly elaborate hiring processes. The medical director or chairperson of the recruitment committee identifies those applicants whose paper credentials (training, board certification or board eligibility, and letters of reference) are acceptable, verifies those credentials, and then interviews the most promising prospects. The most selective HMOs arrange for candidates to be interviewed by several plan physicians in addition to the medical director. Before hiring, these plans insist on telephone references (because they are more apt to reveal useful information than are letters) and track down any prior problems the applicant may have had with licensure, hospital privileges, and physical or psychological impairment.

Often, HMOs recruit on a national basis. Physicians in charge of recruitment place advertisements in medical journals, call directors of hospital residency programs for names of suitable candidates, and draw on the informal medical network of their plan's physicians.

Independent practice associations. Depending on the way in which an IPA is organized, physicians may be selected by a medical director working for the HMO side of the organization, by a loosely organized physician association that contracts with the HMO, or by a number of individual physician groups who contract with the plan. In general, IPA model HMOs do not have as elaborate a selection process as do group practice plans.

The meticulousness of the review process may vary, depending on the sponsorship of the plan. One that has been organized by a hospital will generally accept all physicians who have satisfied the hospital's credentialing process. One that is organized by a county medical society will usually accept all physicians who are members. Plans organized by insurance companies may have a credentialing process that is quite thorough or one that simply checks to make sure that the physician has a valid license and carries an appropriate level of malpractice insurance. The most selective plans evaluate the quality of outpatient care that prospective physicians provide.

In a network model plan, in which the HMO contracts with a number of established group practices, the selection and credentialing will probably have been performed by each individual group. Although a group will, in most cases, do a thorough evaluation of applicants who wish to join, some HMOs insist on doing their own credentialing of new physicians joining the group.

A good group practice plan will have an extensive evaluation process for new physicians. There is often a probationary period that lasts from twelve to twenty-four months. During this period, the new physician's work is monitored to make sure he or she practices high-quality medicine and relates well to patients.

How HMOs Monitor Medical Care

HMOs that have been certified by the state or the federal government are required to have formal programs to evaluate the quality of office and hospital practice. This continual monitoring of physicians makes it possible to identify and correct substandard care and to improve medical quality. This is one of the most valuable, if least-promoted, features of HMO medical care.

Because it is impossible to examine every single physician-patient interaction, quality assessment programs establish standards of good care and then evaluate how well the plan's physicians live up to those standards. A carefully designed program inspects the training and credentials of those who give medical care, the precision with which they document what they have done, the suitability of the tests they order, and the effectiveness of the treatments they recommend. Just as a physician evaluates a patient's overall health by looking at a few key indicators—temperature, urine, skin tone, blood pressure, and so on—a quality assessment program identifies key factors that will indicate the performance of a medical system: the rate of cesarean section, readmission to the hospital within thirty days for the same problem, follow-up of abnormal pap smears or high blood pressure readings. A good program is designed not only to gather data but also to recommend improvements and find out whether those improvements have been made. A plan that is serious about medical quality will place responsibility for its quality assurance program at a high level of the organization, and the program should be reviewed annually by its board of directors.

In contrast, indemnity insurance plans do no selecting, credentialing, or monitoring of physicians, except to look for fraud in billings. Although large, reputable group practices have quality assurance programs and hospitals monitor the quality of care provided in their institutions, there are currently no effective systems to monitor the care provided by independent physicians in their offices.

Protection for HMO Members

Certification. Most HMOs undergo inspection by an outside agency to determine whether a given plan meets that agency's standards both for good medical care and for sound business practices. This type of inspection does not exist for other kinds of insurance carriers or for the physicians who provide care to people covered by their plans. Most plans have had their operations reviewed either under a state certification program or by the federal government and, often, by both. There are a number of sources of HMO certification: governmental agencies, including the federal Office of Prepaid Health Care (OPHC) and state agencies, and two private organizations: the Accreditation Association for Ambulatory Health Care, Inc., and the National Committee on Quality Assurance (NCQA).

Financial protection for members. A properly organized HMO has contracts with physicians and hospitals that, even in the case of the HMO's insolvency, forbid them to bill HMO members directly for covered services provided while the HMO was in operation. All federally qualified HMOs must have such contracts and, in addition, must ensure that in the event of financial failure of the plan, all medical bills that members incur for one month after the HMO goes out of business will be paid.

Although a number of HMOs have failed financially, in almost all cases the plans were acquired by larger HMOs that absorbed their losses and provided continuity of care and coverage to the HMOs' members. To protect members of failing HMOs, some states now require all HMOs in the community to accept all members from failing plans. If your state has no such law, or if there are no other HMOs available, those who have signed up through an employer can transfer to one of the other insurance plans the employer offers. If you joined the HMO as an individual, you could be left without insurance.

Do HMOs Provide High Quality Care and Service?

If you are unfamiliar with HMOs, you may wonder about the level of care and service these organizations provide. In general, studies of medical quality have demonstrated that their performance matches or exceeds the level of medical care provided by physicians in a fee-for-service setting. Studies of consumer satisfaction show that HMOs compare favorably in many areas of care and service.

Medical quality. In 1979 researchers at Johns Hopkins School of Public Health reviewed twenty-five studies that compared the quality of medicine practiced in prepaid plans with that found in the community as a whole. Nineteen of the studies concluded that the care in prepaid plans was superior to what was available in the community; six found it to be as good. No study found HMO care to be in any way inferior.[10]

The most extensive study of a single HMO was organized by The RAND Corporation, and the results were released in 1987. This study found that members of Group Health Cooperative of Puget Sound, a large group practice plan, were 28 percent less expensive to care for than a control group who saw fee-for-service doctors—but were just as healthy. The study concludes that "the cost savings achieved by this HMO through lowering hospitalization rates were not reflected in lower levels of health status."[11]

The most recent comprehensive study of quality was released in 1986 by the Federal Office of Technology Assessment. It compared prepaid with fee-for-service physicians and found that the quality of care in prepaid groups was "at least as good and usually better than that of comparison groups." The study also found that prepaid plans "have had higher percentages of board-certified physicians, for example; have followed standards for process of care as well as or better than fee-for-service physicians; and have had comparable or better morbidity and mortality rates."[12]

Consumer satisfaction. People who belong to HMOs are, on balance, slightly more satisfied with their care and coverage than those who are not members. A 1984 Louis Harris survey found that 48 percent of HMO members nationwide described themselves as "very satisfied" with the health care services they received, as opposed to 34 percent of eligible nonmembers (people who could have chosen an HMO and did not). Ninety percent of HMO members reported satisfaction with their doctors. The figure for eligible nonmembers was 85 percent. Eighty-six percent of HMO members were satisfied with their ability to see a doctor when they needed one, as compared with 78 percent of eligible nonmembers. HMO members were also more satisfied with waiting times to get physician appointments than were eligible nonmembers: 69 percent compared to 59 percent. When it came to hospital services, rates of satisfaction were similar; 76 percent of HMO members were satisfied as compared with 75 percent of eligible nonmembers. HMO members were slightly more dissatisfied than nonmembers with access to specialists: 15 percent of HMO members were dissatisfied compared with 13 percent of eligible nonmembers.[13]

Of course, these numbers reflect the experiences of a self-selected group. How satisfied would random people be with an HMO? As part of The RAND Corporation's large-scale study of prepaid medical care, researchers surveyed a group of participants who were assigned to a group practice HMO, even though they had previously chosen to receive care in the fee-for-service setting. After one year, these people were less satisfied with several aspects of the HMO, including length of waits for appointments and continuity of care than the group that continued to receive care in a fee-for-service setting. They were, however, more satisfied than the latter group with length of office waits and the cost of care. After three years, there was no overall difference in satisfaction between the group that had been assigned to the HMO and those who had self-selected an HMO.[14]

3

Good Medical Care and How to Get It

Buried in the dry and tedious language of an insurance policy is a set of rules that will affect the way you get medical care. Depending on its structure, a given plan may enhance or undermine your ability to get the care you want. Therefore, we suggest that you consider your own definition of good medical care before you select a policy.

Which Is Better: "More" or "Less"?

When it comes to defining good medical care, physicians and patients usually prefer one of two basic approaches. To determine which one best describes your own attitudes, ask yourself these questions:

1. Do I believe that a complete annual physical, with a full series of screening tests, is extremely important?
2. When I have puzzling symptoms, do I expect to have a variety of laboratory tests to make sure that I am okay?
3. If I had a minor medical complaint, would I be annoyed with a physician who was reluctant to give me medication and instead suggested that my body would heal itself?

Would I prefer to walk out of the doctor's office with a prescription?
4. If I were to develop a worrisome ailment, would I prefer going directly to a specialist rather than first seeing a primary care physician?

"Yes" answers to most of these questions put you in the "more is better" category. People in this category generally want treatment of some type when they are ill, and are sometimes willing to try a new drug or undergo surgery rather than take a wait-and-see approach to their problems. Often, they favor a more aggressive specialist-oriented approach to medical care over the more conservative approach used by most primary care physicians.

If, on the other hand, you answered "no" to most of the questions above, you belong to the "less is better" school of thought. People in this group tend to use medical services cautiously, and they prefer to let nature do the healing whenever possible.

In truth, "just enough" health care is best. But "just enough" may be defined in very different ways. In *Medicine and Culture*, Lynn Payer describes how treatment varies according to the underlying cultural assumptions of a given country. "American medicine is aggressive," Payer observes. "American doctors perform more diagnostic tests than doctors in France, West Germany, or England. They often eschew drug treatment in favor of more aggressive surgery, but if they do use drugs they are likely to use higher doses and more aggressive drugs. While official recommendations as to dose are often higher than those given in other countries, even when official recommendations drop many doctors continue to believe that higher doses will be better."[1]

The problems of overtreatment are a matter of growing concern among our leading medical thinkers. Marcia Angell, M.D., senior deputy editor of *The New England Journal of Medicine*, asserts that "much of the medical care in this country is unnecessary—by which I mean that it is of no demonstrated value to those who receive it—and some of it is harmful."[2]

Kerr L. White, M.D., former deputy director for health sciences of the Rockefeller Foundation, supports this view. "Although things are much better than they were a generation ago, it is still the case that only about 15 percent of all contemporary clinical interventions are supported by objective scientific evidence that they do more good than harm."[3]

Defensive Medicine Is Not Good Medicine

American patients reinforce this cultural tendency to overtreat. Physicians have learned that many malpractice suits arise because a test or treatment that might have been ordered was omitted. Many doctors now practice "defensive medicine," a phrase that describes the ordering of tests and procedures in order to prevent patients from suing or from winning lawsuits if they do sue. Patients seldom complain of *overtreatment* or bring suit because of it. They may be unhappy that a particular treatment was ineffective, but they rarely ask the kinds of questions beforehand that might help them avoid the risk and expense of an unnecessary test or treatment. Very few understand that the treatment that did not work well often should never have been done at all.

For example, if your five-year-old son falls off a swing and hits his head, your physician might order skull films even though the child is fine, never lost consciousness, and doesn't have any bruises or swelling. If, the next day, your son should develop a subdural hematoma (an expanding blood clot under the skull), require neurosurgery, and suffer brain damage, you would not be able to claim that the doctor failed to perform an adequate evaluation. Or, if you are in labor and the fetal monitor suggests there may be problems, the obstetrician who practices defensive medicine will often perform a cesarean section, even though the abnormal readings are not conclusive. If the baby is abnormal, the doctor will have "done everything possible."

The problem with defensive medicine is that it is for the doctor's protection, not the patient's benefit. Studies have shown that routine skull films on all head injuries are unnecessary and that the practice of performing cesarean sections on all women with abnormal fetal monitor readings leads to unnecessary surgery that subjects mother and child to risk.[4]

In truth, a better phrase might be "offensive medicine." If you are given an X ray you don't need, you have been exposed to radiation with no benefit to offset it. If fetal monitoring leads to a cesarean section, you may have undergone the risks of surgery for no good reason. Such attacks on a patient's health for a doctor's legal protection are offensive.

Defensive medicine is also expensive medicine. A survey of physicians conducted by *Medical Economics* revealed that 63 percent of respondents included the expense of legal self-protection in their fees, at a median annual cost of $20,020 per physician. For specialties at highest risk for expensive malpractice judgments, such as obstetrics and neurosurgery, the yearly cost passed on to patients for defensive tactics could be as high as $100,000, not including the physician's actual malpractice premiums, which are also factored into the fee.[5]

If you are concerned that your physician may be practicing defensive medicine at your expense, ask why you need a given test or procedure. If the doctor answers vaguely or says, "Just to be sure," be prepared to ask further questions. "Just to be sure of what? What will happen if I don't have this test today? How likely am I to have this problem? What are the risks with this procedure?"

A doctor who is ordering a test for your benefit will have specific answers to your questions. If, however, the answers leave you unconvinced, tell the physician that you are unwilling to have the test. Of course, you must be prepared to change physicians if he or she is unwilling to treat you without the results of the test.

Good Medical Care Is Conservative

Whether you receive care from a fee-for-service doctor or from one who is in prepaid practice, you need to know how to evaluate the quality of care you receive. We believe the best doctors are "conservative," a term of high praise bestowed by physicians on colleagues who are judicious in their use of medical technology and who rigorously apply the Hippocratic injunction: First do no harm.

To visualize a conservative approach to medical care, take a look at Figure 1. "Health Status" is plotted along the vertical axis of the graph and "Amount of Health Care" along the horizontal. When you look at the curve, you will notice that people with medical problems who receive no health care have a poor health status. When they first receive care, their health status line soars, but with additional care, the climb is less dramatic. Eventually, additional increments of care result in almost no measurable improvement (point A) and in some cases may cause the health status line to decline (point B). A doctor who continues to order tests and treatments after the health status line flattens out is, in medical parlance, "practicing medicine on the flat part of the curve."

Figure 2 illustrates the case of a woman with untreated high blood pressure. When she first receives treatment (drug A), her health status improves; it continues to improve when the doctor adds a drug (B) and succeeds in bringing the pressure down to nearly normal. With the substitution of a stronger drug (C), however, the pressure improves only slightly, and she now begins to complain of side effects caused by the drugs. Her health status line first flattens out, and then descends as unwanted side effects appear. Physicians who practice conservative medicine avoid the flat part of the curve.

Patients can identify a doctor who practices conservative medicine by noticing whether he or she habitually does the following:

- asks a number of questions before coming to any conclusion
- calls for a few noninvasive tests at first, ordering more ex-

Figure 1

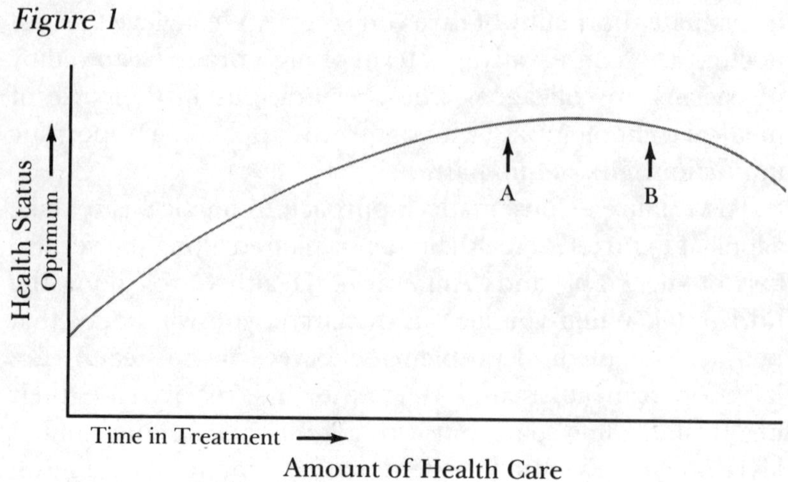

Figure 2

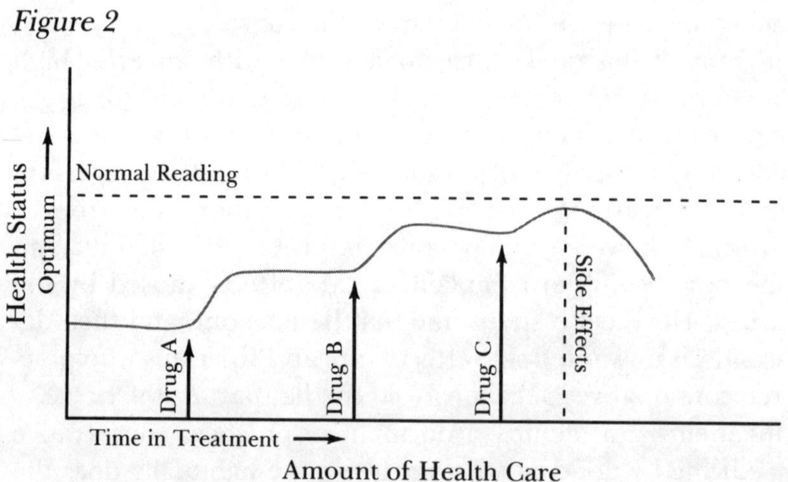

tensive tests or diagnostic procedures only if the results of the first tests are abnormal and the problem is not resolving itself
- discusses alternative approaches before beginning any treatment
- explains all risks thoroughly, welcomes and patiently answers questions, and willingly arranges for another medical opinion before proceeding
- recommends well-established treatments (unless the patient has a very unusual problem or one so severe that it has failed to respond to conventional approaches)

The conservative approach is a sophisticated balancing of risk versus benefit rather than a simple choice between aggressive "more is better" medicine and "less is better" therapeutic nihilism. Sometimes speedy intervention to prevent more serious problems is the conservative choice. Appendicitis, for example, must be treated promptly or the appendix may perforate, causing a dangerous complication called peritonitis. Surgeons who are too aggressive will operate too often, needlessly exposing some of their patients to the risk of surgery; surgeons who are overly cautious will elect not to operate immediately in some cases where immediate surgery was called for, thus exposing some of their patients to the risks of peritonitis.

Must You Always Have a Diagnosis?

Conservative physicians do not always pursue a definitive diagnosis. In *Matters of Life and Death*, Eugene Robin, M.D., an educator and scientist, warns of the consequences of unwarranted invasions of the body: "Diagnostic measures are not invariably accurate or safe, and there is not an effective form of treatment for each diagnosis."[6]

Why do some physicians focus on making a diagnosis at the expense of the patient? The answer lies in the way medical students are trained. Most of their time is spent working in hospitals, taking care of very sick people under the tutelage of professors who place a constant and unrelenting emphasis on making the correct diagnosis. During this period of training, they are often criticized for failing to perform enough tests.

In the real world of office medicine, however, most problems resolve themselves, or require minimal treatment. Suppose, for example, that you are experiencing some burning sensations in your stomach that improve after eating. Your physician will consider the two likeliest causes: hyperacidity or a duodenal ulcer. You can undergo diagnostic X rays of the stomach and duodenum that will reveal whether or not you have an ulcer, or you can take antacids for a brief period to find out whether your symptoms will be relieved. If the antacids are effective, you will have avoided expense, effort, and unnecessary exposure to X rays.

Sometimes patients are as anxious as their physicians for a diagnosis, regardless of its utility. Howard M. Spiro, M.D., a well-known professor at Yale University School of Medicine, posed the antacid question to a group of nonphysician colleagues and was surprised by how many "were frightened at the thought that *their* physician would not immediately try to pinpoint the physical cause of every complaint, regardless of cost. Rule out cancer first, and then worry about my worries!" He found he could not convince them that "the outcome would be changed little by that short detour."[7]

Tests do not produce an exact answer; they are often less than 100 percent accurate and generate both "false positive" (the test says you have a disease when you don't) and "false negative" (the test says you are normal when you are not) results. Most people may not be aware of the dangers that arise when a false positive leads to a single-minded hunt for the definitive diagnosis. Dr. Eugene Robin illustrates this problem with the sad tale of a healthy seventy-eight-year-old woman who developed a respiratory infection.

> The infection may have been bronchitis, a relatively minor infection of the bronchial tubes, or it may have been pneumonia,

> a more serious infection of the lung tissue. Neither necessarily requires hospitalization. She was nevertheless admitted to a hospital and during routine testing of her blood was found to have a low potassium level. Although he observed no obvious manifestations of potassium deficiency, her physician prescribed potassium to be administered by vein. . . . A potassium solution was administered to this patient, but with inadequate monitoring. Her heart stopped, and a post-mortem examination of the blood showed that she had almost certainly died of potassium intoxication.[8]

Because they are aware of problems caused by inaccurate tests results, conservative physicians do not encourage patients to take an elaborate battery of screening tests. According to the U.S. Preventive Services Task Force, only a few tests are worth doing routinely on healthy people *with no special risk factors* in their medical history:[9]

- a blood pressure check every year or two
- a pap test for women every one to three years, once three consecutive annual paps have produced normal results
- a periodic measurement of cholesterol for middle-aged men (every five years or so)
- a test for blood in the stool every one or two years after the age of fifty for people with known risk factors for colorectal cancer
- mammograms every one or two years for all women over age fifty and perhaps regular mammograms for women over age thirty-five if they have a mother or sister who was diagnosed with breast cancer before she reached menopause[10]

Guidelines have changed for routine screening tests on hospital patients. In the past, most physicians ordered electrocardiograms, chest X rays, and biochemical profiles (blood tests) for every patient they admitted to the hospital, no matter what the reason for the admission. A number of studies have now shown that there is no benefit to doing any of these tests unless they are related to the specific problem causing the hospitalization.[11]

Basic Principles of Conservative Medicine

Annual physicals are unnecessary if you are healthy. Numerous studies have shown that annual physicals do not reliably uncover hidden but treatable problems in people who have no symptoms. By 1983, this body of research prompted the Council on Scientific Affairs of the American Medical Association to release a report titled "Medical Evaluations of Healthy Persons." In it, the council recommends a routine physical examination every five years from age twenty to sixty, and every two years thereafter, except for certain screening tests, such as pap smears and blood pressure measurements, which should be done more frequently.[12]

Unnecessary surgery is common. A recent study found that there were twenty-two admissions per 1,000 people per year for discretionary surgery in people covered by an indemnity plan as compared to only seven per 1,000 in an HMO. There was no difference in health outcomes between the two groups.[13] Another study compared thirty hospital market areas in Maine and found that some had 3.5 times the rate of hysterectomies as others, with no evidence that there was any greater need for those procedures in the areas that had high rates.[14]

A hospital is not a good place to be unless you really need to be there. Hospitals pose substantial hazards to patients, who risk hospital-acquired infections and errors in administering medications, and endure an atmosphere that is attuned more to the needs and schedules of staff than to the needs of patients.

One major study found that 36 percent of patients admitted to a university hospital contracted hospital-acquired infections.[15] The patients who suffered these complications were for the most part older, used more medications, and had longer lengths of stay than the rest of the patient population. Another study, one that focused on people age seventy-five or older, found that 38 percent experienced hospital-acquired complications.[16]

The latest drug may not be the best. In fact, a drug that has been in use for a long time is usually a safer choice. For information about the newest medications, physicians often rely too heavily on the drug company salespeople. Unless a life-threatening condition calls for aggressive or experimental treatment, a conservative physician prefers to use medications that have been thoroughly tested on a large population for a long enough time to disclose risks that may not have been evident during the drug's initial approval process.

All preventive measures are not equally desirable. One of the great and taken-for-granted miracles of modern medicine is the ability to *prevent* disease. It is hard for us today to imagine watching our loved ones suffer and die from the fearful infectious scourges—the typhus, typhoid, cholera, smallpox, and diphtheria epidemics—that laid waste to countless lives just a few decades ago. Now we can either prevent many diseases or detect and successfully treat some of the great killers at an early and curable stage.

But sometimes preventive techniques create more problems than they prevent. There is no scientific evidence that routine fetal monitoring during labor is beneficial, yet it is now so commonly done that it has been the principal contributor to a 150 percent increase in cesarean sections—and their attendant risks to mother and child. In the 1970s, the federal government, fearing a possible swine flu epidemic, urged widespread immunizations. That epidemic never occurred, but hundreds of people suffered severe complications from the flu vaccine, and some died.

To sort out the useful techniques from those of questionable value, ask the following questions before you decide to have a test, take a medication, or undergo surgery:

Questions to Ask Your Doctor about Screening Tests

1. Why do I need this test? Am I in a high-risk age group or situation?
2. Have studies shown that this test is an effective indicator of a problem for someone of my age and sex, or in my special situation?
3. How accurate is this test? What are the chances of re-

ceiving a false positive or false negative result?

4. Where will this test be performed? What is the quality of the laboratory and what are the credentials of the technicians who work there?
5. What are the risks associated with this test?
6. If the results are abnormal, would I need further tests or would I need treatment?
7. Would further tests be invasive and risky?
8. What treatment would this test lead to if the results were abnormal? (And ask yourself if you would accept that treatment.)
9. What are the risks from not having the test?
10. If my symptoms make a given diagnosis likely, would there be any advantage in skipping the test and proceeding directly to treatment?

Questions to Ask Your Doctor about Medications

1. Do I definitely have the disease this drug is supposed to treat?
2. What are the risks and side effects of this medication?
3. What will this medication do for me? Will it cure my disease or only treat symptoms? (If it will only treat symptoms and has significant risks, ask yourself whether you still want to take it.)
4. If it will cure my disease, is that cure worth the risks and/or side effects of taking the drug?
5. Has this drug been in general and widespread use? Are its effects, risks, and side effects well established?
6. Does this drug come in different forms?
7. If there are different formulations, what are the advantages and disadvantages? For example, would I be better off taking an oral form, a patch, an aerosol, or a cream?
8. Am I better off with a drug I take once a day, twice a day, four times a day?
9. Can I save money by taking a generic form of the drug?
10. If there is a difference between the generic and the

brand-name drug, is that difference one of efficacy or one of convenience? (If the benefit is one of convenience, ask yourself whether it's worth the extra money.)

11. What kinds of side effects should I be alert to after I've started taking the drug? Should I stop taking it if I notice them?
12. (Ask the pharmacist the following:) Is there a special way to take the drug? Are there any precautions I should observe while I am taking it? If the drug has side effects, is there any way I can minimize them?

Questions to Ask Your Doctor about Surgical Procedures

1. Why do I need to have this procedure done?
2. What are the risks of this operation?
3. Have studies shown this procedure to be effective for someone of my age and sex and in my particular situation?
4. What has been your experience in doing this procedure? How many patients have you performed it on? What percentage of these patients have had a successful outcome?
5. Is there an alternative to surgery? Have nonsurgical treatments shown results comparable to surgery?
6. Do I need this procedure immediately or can it wait? If it can wait, for how long would it be safe to delay it?
7. What will happen to me if I do not have this procedure?
8. Will this procedure be performed in a hospital, a physician's office, or an outpatient facility?
9. Is this procedure done under local, regional, or general anesthesia, and what are the risks of each form of anesthesia that could be used?
10. How will this procedure affect the quality of my life if it succeeds? If it fails?
11. What is the fee for this procedure, and how will my insurance cover it?
12. Will you help me determine how my insurance policy covers this procedure, so I can make sure that I am reim-

bursed? Must I get a second opinion? Must this procedure be performed in a particular type of facility? Will I have to get prior authorization from my insurance carrier? What will happen if the insurance company refuses to approve the procedure?

The Importance of Primary Care

The best medical care begins with the services of a personal physician who is a generalist, or "primary care" physician, trained to shed a floodlight on a broad range of medical problems and to enlist the expertise of specialists when needed. A primary care physician knows that in the world of outpatient practice most symptoms go away by themselves. He or she will be alert to your individual way of responding to sickness, will notice whether you are alarmed by symptoms or downplay them, and will take into account your family and work situation. When you are sick or need medical advice, he or she is the first person to consult. Physicians trained to offer primary care may be family practitioners, general internists, pediatricians, or specialists in adolescent medicine.

If primary care is like a floodlight, illuminating the widest range of ailments, specialty care is like a spotlight, a narrow and intense beam shed on complicated or unusual medical problems. The in-depth knowledge of the specialist is also a crucial element of good medical care, but that knowledge is most valuable when it is applied to the correct case and at the correct time.

Overtreatment and the risks that accompany unnecessary medical care often occur because specialists are called on to provide care more appropriate to the skills of a generalist. This point is brought home by a gastroenterologist who left his position on the faculty of a medical school to start his own private practice:

> The people I saw at the medical school were referred to me because they had serious underlying problems, so when my new

private practice patients came in and said they were worried because they had diarrhea, I would set out in pursuit of a diagnosis, as I had been trained and had taught others; and I would perform the kinds of elaborate and often invasive studies I was used to doing in my medical school practice. Fortunately, most of my patients got better despite my aggressive approach.[17]

In his faculty practice, he saw only those patients who had been screened. By the time he saw a patient with diarrhea, that condition would have persisted for weeks, despite treatment by the primary care physician. What he didn't know about in his faculty post, because he didn't see them, were all the patients who recovered with little or no treatment.

Going to a specialist when you truly need one is a part of high-quality health care. But an unnecessary visit to a specialist may be *more* dangerous to your health than the risk that a generalist might misdiagnose your problem. Specialists may also make a wrong diagnosis and, given the types of serious problems they are trained to deal with, may be inclined to recommend tests and treatments, with their associated risks, that go far beyond what's needed to correctly diagnose and effectively treat the problem.

How Primary Care Doctors Work with Specialists

Whether they work in a fee-for-service practice or a managed care setting, primary care physicians can help you get better, more cost-effective specialty care, and they can help you avoid care you do not need. They do this in a number of ways.

They can choose the right specialist for your particular problem. If you had a back problem and decided to seek a medical specialist, would you choose a neurologist, a neurosurgeon, an orthopedist, a physiatrist, or a rheumatologist? Would you look for a nonphysician who works with physicians, like a physical therapist, or should you try a less conventional approach and seek out a chiropractor or a licensed therapeutic massage therapist? Or would a biofeedback trainer be the best person to help you?

The answer may depend on the exact nature of your problem, the kinds of specialists available in your community, the level of skill of those specialists, and the physical demands of your occupation. A primary care physician who knows you and your problem can steer you to the most appropriate specialist and will help you avoid undertaking an uncertain, time-consuming, and sometimes expensive search on your own.

They can direct you to well-trained and competent specialists. Some people simply ask friends and relatives for referrals and then rely on their suggestions with no further checking. A study published in *Pediatrics* found that more than 80 percent of families based their choice of physician on one source of information. "Most consulted neighbors or family or relied on their own experience as a patient." Only a few discussed their choice with another physician.[18]

A good primary care physician will be selective in choosing specialists. At a minimum, he or she can make sure that you are referred to one who is fully credentialed. Studies have shown that patients of surgeons who are board-certified have a lower mortality rate than patients of surgeons without that credential.[19]

They can serve as liaisons and coordinators. After you see a specialist, you may have unanswered questions. In some cases, you may see two or more specialists who give you contradictory recommendations. Your primary care physician can help you sort through the various opinions you have received to come up with a sensible treatment plan. In many cases, you can receive care directly from your primary care physician after you have had a consultation with a specialist.

They can make sure the specialist has full information about all your medical problems. If, for example, you have diabetes and need surgery for your gallbladder, your primary care physician can make certain that the surgeon has relevant details about your diabetes. Information about your medications or previous complications may be vitally important to the care you receive during and after surgery.

They can stay involved with your care even though you need to consult a specialist. A physician you have seen for a number of problems over time knows how you react to stress, how you tolerate pain, how your body handles medication. By having a familiar and trusted physician to manage your care, you may also reduce anxiety and help your body heal better and faster. One interesting study found that patients who had had extra education prior to surgery to reduce their anxiety required less postoperative pain medication.[20]

Additional Benefits of Using a Primary Care Physician

An ongoing relationship with a physician is a source of healing. Primary care physicians who take care of patients for a number of ailments develop a relationship with them over time, and research has shown that a good medical relationship pays off in better health. One study looked at a group practice in which reorganization had disturbed patient-physician relationships and found that there was an increase in the number of visits for illness.[21] Another study looked at two groups of patients in a health care clinic: those who were treated by the same physician each time and those who were given care by the first doctor available. Both patients and physicians in the first group reported a higher quality of care compared with the second group.[22]

You may be able to share information more comfortably with a physician you know and trust. Physicians can diagnose 70 to 90 percent of medical problems just by taking a history, but to do this, they rely on your willingness to discuss personal matters honestly and accurately.

You can reduce the risk of undesirable drug interactions by having one provider do the prescribing. A physician who is aware of all your health problems and knows the drugs you are taking will be able to monitor possible harmful combinations more easily than would a series of doctors, each treating you for a separate problem.

You will have a coordinator and advocate if you must enter the hospital. Your primary care physician can make sure that you are given coordinated care from the various doctors and other health professionals you must deal with in the hospital, and he or she can discuss with you or a trusted friend or family member any questions that arise.

You can save money by using a primary care physician. Unless money is no object, or you have unusually comprehensive insurance coverage, you are going to be concerned about the cost of your medical care. A 1989 survey found that the median charge for a first office visit was $34 for a family physician, $40 for a pediatrician, $51 for an internist, $80 for a gastroenterologist, and $101 for a cardiologist.[23] Because specialists tend to perform more tests, the total cost of a visit would be even higher. Furthermore, once your doctor gets to know you, he or she may be willing to give advice on the telephone when appropriate, saving you the expense (not to mention the time and energy) of making an office visit.

Disadvantages of Relying on a Primary Care Physician

You are putting all your eggs in one basket. If you select a poorly trained, or otherwise incompetent, physician, you will receive poor care for all your problems.

You may risk delays in getting the specialty treatment you need. If you have a rash, for example, your primary care physician may try several treatments before he or she decides that you need to consult a dermatologist. In unusual circumstances, a delay may cause your condition to become significantly worse.

Specialty Care and Your Choice of Health Plan

If you plan to rely on a competent primary care physician as the cornerstone of your medical care, both indemnity and managed care plans will be suitable for you. However, if you want the freedom to see a specialist whenever you choose, you will be far happier with an indemnity plan. Some preferred provider plans may prevent you from self-referring to specialists, and almost all health maintenance organizations will insist that referrals to their designated specialists be made through your primary care HMO physician.

Choosing a Good Physician

Good physicians possess two kinds of skills: technical and interpersonal. On the technical side, they take thorough health histories and keep careful written records of their findings, recommendations, and treatment plans on the patient's chart. They perform careful physical exams and discuss risks and benefits before recommending a diagnostic procedure or treatment. When appropriate, they refer their patients to competent specialists, but they are willing to stay involved if patients need their advice. When they choose medical services, they pick laboratories and hospitals with the highest standards.

The most effective physicians also possess certain important human qualities. According to Gordon Deckert, M.D., a well-known physician educator, the doctors who achieve the best medical results, no matter what their specialty, are those who communicate their concern in a helpful way, explain medical matters clearly, and involve their patients in problem-solving.

You as a patient can influence the quality of the care you receive. You can begin by choosing physicians carefully. Once you have found a physician you respect, you can help to build an open and ongoing relationship by providing thorough information about your medical history, answering the doctor's questions honestly, and voicing your own worries and concerns, taking careful note of symptoms and their onset, asking questions about tests, medications, and procedures, and conscientiously following treatment plans.

Primary Care Physicians

You will probably choose your primary care physician from one of the following four specialties, each with its particular strengths and areas of expertise.

Specialist in family medicine. A doctor in this specialty has had three years of very broad post-medical school training that includes pediatrics, adult medicine, obstetrics, gynecology, geriatrics, emergency medicine, and orthopedics. A family physician is educated in couple counseling and family counseling, and trained to observe problems in family dynamics caused by an illness. Those family medicine specialists who practice obstetrics can, because of their broad training, provide care that extends beyond pregnancy and childbirth. After the baby is born, they can continue to offer medical care to both mother and child.

General internist. A physician in this specialty has had three years of post-medical school training devoted to studying the medical problems relating to the organ systems of adults. A general internist's curriculum will have emphasized cardiology, gastroenterology, endocrinology, rheumatology, hematology, nephrology, and pulmonology. He or she will have had some training in gynecology, counseling, and the medical problems associated with pregnancy but almost none in pediatrics and the treatment of injuries. A handful of general internists take additional training in ambulatory care or behavioral medicine, fields that emphasize the outpatient aspects of medical care.

Internal medicine subspecialists. These internists have taken two or more years of extra training and are sometimes referred to by their colleagues as "ologists," because they have titles like gastroenterologist, rheumatologist, and cardiologist. Some limit their work to their subspecialty area and serve as primary care physicians only to those patients who have significant medical problems in their area of specialization.

Pediatrician. This doctor is extensively trained to give health care to children from birth through puberty. In recent years, some instruction in problems of adolescents has been added to the pediatricians' curriculum, but studies have shown that many general pediatricians are uncomfortable treating teenagers.[24]

Some pediatricians take additional training in child development and behavioral pediatrics. If you want guidance on the emotional aspects of child-rearing, this extra expertise could be quite helpful.

Specialist in adolescent medicine. This is a new kind of primary care physician, one skilled in dealing with the problems of young people in their teens and early twenties. Specialists in adolescent medicine may be pediatricians, family physicians, or occasionally internists, all of whom have taken additional training in normal adolescent development (both physical and emotional) as well as in the treatment of such problems as eating disorders, substance abuse, depression, and suicidal behavior.

This specialty is still too new to have developed the system of testing and certification that distinguishes older specialty areas, but physicians who are serious in their commitment to this age group will usually be members of the Society for Adolescent Medicine (SAM), and many will have taken a fellowship in adolescent medicine. (Pediatricians specializing in this area should, at a minimum, belong to the Adolescent Section of the American Academy of Pediatrics.)

Because teenagers resent being treated like children, they may resist seeing their "baby doctor," and they may be reluctant to reveal important information about their health. Pediatricians who are sensitive to their adolescent patients' concerns will give them confidential and respectful care and offer special hours or a separate waiting room.[25]

Mid-Level Practitioners (MLPs)

Physician assistants, nurse practitioners, and certified nurse-midwives, often referred to as Mid-Level Practitioners, are playing an increasingly important and visible role in medical practice. Most of these providers work in tandem with physicians, giving routine care and providing patient education either in fee-for-service offices or in health care organizations. Well-trained MLPs know the scope of their own abilities and will call on the services of a physician when necessary. They are often particularly knowledgeable about—and more interested in—such commonplace problems as vaginitis or diaper rash, or that large category of bothersome injuries the medical profession refers to as "strains and sprains," and they usually have more time to spend on patient education and answering questions than do physicians.

How do you know if a nurse practitioner or physician assistant is well trained and well supervised? Since programs to train MLPs and state licensing requirements vary widely, your best guarantee is the homework you do in selecting a physician. Good doctors and good medical organizations are selective about all their medical personnel, and they are careful in checking credentials and references. If you prefer to receive care from a physician, though, make your preference known. We believe this is a personal choice and that it should be respected by your physician or health care organization.

Nurse practitioners. This term describes registered nurses who have had additional training, usually at a master's degree level and often in a particular field such as obstetrics, women's health care, pediatrics, or geriatrics; they can examine, diagnose, and treat a given range of medical problems. Some nurse practitioners specialize in "family practice" and are trained to care for a number of minor and chronic problems that afflict all age groups. Each state has its own laws governing their licensure, but in most states they can write prescriptions (except for addictive or narcotic drugs). Some states allow nurse practitioners to practice independently, but unless you live in a community where physicians are unavailable, we recommend that you select a physician whom you can see if you become seriously ill.

Certified nurse-midwives. These are registered nurses with additional obstetrics training who have graduated from a program approved by their national organization, The American College of Nurse-Midwives. They must have an ongoing arrangement with a physician who is available to provide backup obstetrical care in case problems arise. We recommend you use only those midwives who have this credential, since state licensing standards are quite variable.

Physician assistants. These MLPs are college graduates with health care experience who complete a two-year program that includes the same basic sciences taught to medical students (biochemistry, physiology, pharmacology, pathology) plus intensive clinical training in hospitals and physicians' offices. They are employed either by a physician, who directly supervises their work, or by an institution, which will assign a physician as a supervisor. Some states allow physician assistants in rural communities to practice without direct physician supervision, but they are then required to identify a physician who is available to them for consultation on the telephone, or for referral.

Like nurse practitioners, they may choose to specialize in a particular area of medicine or to be a generalist. Many of those who specialize choose to work in surgical areas such as orthopedics, and they are trained to set fractures, treat sprains and strains, and assist in the operating room.

Which Type of Primary Care Practitioner Should You Choose?

Much depends on your personal preference, and therefore we can offer only some general suggestions. Adults might consider either a specialist in family medicine or a general internist. Parents with young children might lean toward choosing a family physician, whereas adults with serious chronic medical problems might prefer an internist.

As a rule, you should not choose a subspecialist to provide your ongoing primary care, but there are exceptions. Adults with complicated or rare medical problems might prefer to get most of their medical care from the subspecialist who is treating them. For example, people with difficult thyroid problems might wish to get as much medical care as possible from their endocrinologist. In such cases, a good solution would be to look for a physician with substantial experience as a generalist and advanced training in a subspecialty area.

For children, either a family physician or a pediatrician would be a good choice. If the adults in the family get their care from an internist, they might turn to a pediatrician for their children's care. Parents who see a family physician for their own care might find it convenient to have their children see the same doctor. Children with such serious problems as diabetes, asthma, or birth injuries who receive primary care from family physicians should be referred to pediatricians or pediatric subspecialists if they develop complications.

For teenagers, the choice of primary care giver is less obvious. If there is no trained specialist in adolescent medicine in your community, your best bet might be a family physician who is skillful in working with young people.

Special concerns for women. In the past, women have experienced great difficulties in receiving true primary care, since many physicians who were otherwise generalists did not offer routine gynecology. Now, women who want to receive all their care from one physician can choose a specialist in family medicine. If you are a woman who prefers to use a general internist, you need to ask whether he or she gives gynecological care, including breast examinations. Many internists do; some don't.

Women who are generally healthy sometimes question why they need a primary care physician at all. Why not simply find a good obstetrician-gynecologist and leave it at that? The problem with this approach is that OBGYNs are not trained to give comprehensive primary care.

Because many of their patients do not receive general medical care, some conscientious OBGYNs have added periodic blood pressure checks and abdominal exams to the usual gynecological and breast exam, and these services provide a real benefit to the woman who has no other source of medical care. Nevertheless, we recommend that ongoing primary care be given by physicians with broader training.

Gender and your choice of provider. Men tend to prefer male physicians and, because a majority of physicians are male, they encounter no problems finding them. Women who wish to use female providers are having an easier time locating them as more and more women doctors emerge from medical training. Some women are content to consult a male physician for gynecological care; others are not. Teenage girls are often more relaxed with a woman provider. If you have been looking without success for a woman physician, you might settle for a male physician who works with a gynecological nurse practitioner.

Special concerns for older adults. Both internists and specialists in family medicine are trained to give medical care to older adults. Some physicians seek further training and attend special programs that focus on geriatric care. If you're trying to find a physician who is sensitive to the special emotional and financial concerns of the elderly as well as to their purely medical needs, you might ask friends if they would recommend their own doctors. If you know someone who works in a nursing home, he or she may have experience in dealing with the physicians who make rounds there and may be able to provide names of those who seem particularly attentive to their patients' needs.

What Resources Are Available to Help You Pick a Good Doctor?

After deciding what kind of physician you are looking for, your next task is to find one who is properly trained and who has an approach and style of practice that suit you. The following guidelines will help you in your search.

Gather names from friends, relatives, neighbors, or co-workers. Ask whether they would recommend their doctors and why. Listen for responses like: "I feel he really listens to me" or "she's always willing to answer my questions." Lay people understandably have difficulty judging technical competence, but they know when they are being treated with respect and concern. Discount responses such as "he's got a lot of famous patients" or "she's so much in demand you have to wait two hours."

If you know any health care professionals, ask them for names. They may have specific suggestions and useful inside information about who the good doctors are. Better still, they may have worked with a number of doctors and have direct knowledge of their abilities, both technical and interpersonal.

Call the hospital with the best reputation in your community, preferably a teaching hospital. Ask for names of affiliated general internists, pediatricians, and specialists in family medicine (if the hospital allows them admitting privileges). The better the hospital, the more carefully it will screen physicians before giving them admitting privileges. Usually, you will simply be given several names taken at random from a list of physicians who have indicated they are accepting new patients. Some hospitals, however, provide information on the physician's age, sex, office location, and special medical interests. If possible, call a teaching hospital—that is, one that is affiliated with a medical school or that offers training programs for interns and residents. Physicians affiliated with teaching hospitals are carefully monitored to ensure that they are well qualified to instruct students and physicians in training.

Determine if the physicians you are considering are board-certified or board-eligible. Students who have satisfactorily completed four years of medical school are given an M.D. degree, but they have very little experience in caring for patients and cannot apply for a state license to practice medicine until they spend at least one year in a combined internship/residency program. Those who have completed a hospital-sponsored training program in their chosen medical specialty are considered board-eligible. They must then pass written and sometimes oral exams in their specialty to become board-certified.

There are twenty-three boards recognized and approved by the American Board of Medical Specialties (ABMS), but there are dozens of other boards that do not meet the qualifications of this organization. ABMS board-certified physicians will be listed in the *ABMS Compendium of Certified Medical Specialists,* a frequently updated reference book available in many public and hospital libraries. The entry for each doctor includes his or her medical school, residency and fellowship training, primary and secondary specialty, and type of practice. Information on an individual physician's certification status is available by calling a toll-free telephone number: 1-800-776-CERT.

In some fields, especially surgical specialties, a physician must perform a certain number of procedures before he or she is allowed to take the board-certification exam. Some doctors never take their boards, and after a certain number of years (depending on the specialty) they are no longer eligible to become board-certified without further training.

Board-eligible physicians who work for a respected group practice have been carefully screened. If you pick a doctor who is part of a well-respected group practice in your community—the Mayo, Cleveland, Lahey, and Ochsner Clinics are nationally famous examples—you might, with confidence, consider a physician who is board-eligible but has not yet taken the board-certification exam.

If you are choosing from a list of HMO physicians, call a service representative of the plan. In general, a high percentage of HMO physicians are board-certified or board-eligible, and the service representative can describe the HMO's selection process and the credentials of particular physicians. Many HMOs, particularly the more tightly controlled group practice models, do rigorous evaluations before they hire.

If you cannot find a board-certified or board-eligible physician, look for one with the best possible credentials. In many rural areas, you will have very limited choice of physicians. Try to find a doctor who has graduated from medical school in the past ten years and has completed a specialty training program in the United States or Canada.

Nontraditional Providers and Quality Care

In addition to physicians, nurse practitioners, and physician assistants, all of whom receive their education and training in hospitals and medical offices—and work closely together—there are many other types of practitioners who are competing for your business. They offer a wide range of services, some excellent and some dubious. Insurance policies vary in the ways they provide coverage of these practitioners' services. Included in this category are osteopaths (doctors of osteopathy) whose training is similar to that of physicians; chiropractors (doctors of chiropractic), who have a far more limited and less standardized training and whose practices vary from useful to fraudulent; and those practitioners such as naturopaths, reflexologists, and iridologists, whom physicians regard as quacks and frauds.

Osteopaths (D.O.s). These practitioners spend four years in a school of osteopathic medicine. After graduating, some D.O.s take specialty training in the same programs as M.D.s and are therefore eligible to become board-certified in a medical specialty by the American Board of Medical Specialties (ABMS). Other osteopaths receive specialty training in osteopathic hospitals and are certified in their specialty by the American Osteopathic Association (A.O.A.). To be members of the Association (as opposed to receiving specialty certification from it) osteopaths must, every three years, demonstrate that they have taken 150 hours of continuing medical education that has been approved by the A.O.A.

Osteopathy is based on a system devised at the end of the last century by Andrew Tayler, a midwestern physician who postulated that disease was caused by obstructed fluids, mainly the blood, and that this obstruction occurred when bones became displaced, particularly those in the spinal column. Healing, as he saw it, was a matter of returning the bones to their proper position and letting nature do the rest of the healing.[26] Although at one time osteopaths and M.D.s were trained very differently, nowadays the only noticeable difference from the patient's point of view might be the fact that the D.O. will treat back problems with spinal manipulation.

If you are interested in choosing an osteopath for a primary care physician, make every effort to find one who is certified by one of the specialty boards of the ABMS. If you cannot, try to find one certified by the A.O.A.

Chiropractors (D.C.s). Members of this profession are not adequately trained to treat medical problems, and they should never serve as primary care providers. They should not be used to treat anything other than acute problems involving the back, neck, and extremities. Monthly preventive spinal manipulations, for example, are financially beneficial to the practitioner but have never been scientifically demonstrated to be useful to the patient. Some chiropractors make claims that are clearly fraudulent and offer treatments that are useless at best and dangerous at worst. High colonic irrigations, for example, a favorite treatment with some unscrupulous chiropractors, are medically indefensible.

The field of chiropractic is based on the theory that almost all medical problems emanate from abnormalities of the spine. Practitioners are given extensive training in treating back and neck problems with different types of manipulation, and many states restrict their practice to these types of treatment. Such treatments, however, may be very effective. The conservative physicians of *The Harvard Medical School Health Letter*, in a review of the field, stated that "studies suggest that chiropractic adjustments provide more immediate reduction of pain than placebo treatments, and they often appear to produce speedier improvement than standard medical approaches."[27]

Insurance coverage of chiropractors varies, sometimes as a function of their political power in a given area. Before seeking care from them, make sure to check your health insurance policy.

Other nontraditional providers. This catch-all category—including naturopaths, reflexologists, iridologists, homeopaths, and clinical ecologists—is enjoying an upswing in popularity. Ironically, this interest coincides with a rapid increase in effective medical treatments for a greater range of problems. Certain portions of nontraditional providers' theories may have scientific validity and their services may be helpful in some cases—if the practitioners use only noninvasive techniques and make sure that their patients consult physicians for any problem that scientific medicine can treat.

Nevertheless, we strongly recommend that you avoid such practitioners for your health care. Instead, we urge you to find a properly trained physician who is responsive to your interest in these nontraditional forms of treatment. Often, these physicians belong to the American Holistic Medical Association, to which you can write for names of member physicians in your area (2727 Fairview Avenue E., Seattle, Washington 98102).

Choosing Mental Health Professionals with the Right Credentials

When it comes to mental health care, judgments are inevitably subjective, and it is difficult to determine the quality of care you are receiving. Your best strategy in finding a qualified mental health specialist is to look for a professional that falls into one of the following groups.

Psychiatrists. These are physicians (M.D.s) with specialty training in mental illness. Psychiatrists specialize in treating psychological problems that require medication (they are the only mental health professionals who can prescribe medication) or hospitalization. Psychiatrists also provide psychotherapy for a broad range of emotional problems, but they are not necessarily better trained to do so than are other professionals in the mental health field.

Clinical psychologists. These practitioners hold a doctoral degree (Ph.D. or Psy.D.) from an approved program that requires four years of postgraduate study, plus another year or two of residency training. Clinical psychologists (as opposed to educational, experimental, or other types of psychologists) are well trained to provide psychotherapy and may also be skilled in administering a variety of psychological tests that are helpful in diagnosis and treatment.

Clinical social workers. These are therapists who hold a master's degree in social work (M.S.W.), obtained after a two-year postgraduate program. Most clinical social workers work for organizations (hospitals, HMOs, institutes) or with a psychiatrist or psychologist, and their fees tend to be lower than those of psychiatrists or psychologists. They may have extra training in such areas as chemical dependency treatment or family therapy.

Psychiatric nurses. These practitioners are registered nurses (R.N.s) who have received substantial extra training. Most psychiatric nurses are employed in hospitals; some work with psychiatrists.

Unless you are referred by a practitioner from one of the categories above, or by your physician, it is best to avoid therapists with Ph.D.s and M.A.s in fields other than those specified above. Many people have earned degrees in areas of psychology other than clinical work, but no matter how impressive their credentials may sound, you cannot assume they have received adequate training to provide therapy. Similarly, those people with an M.A. in psychology or in counseling do not have sufficient training to qualify as therapists.

Steer clear of self-styled specialists in mental health. Anyone can print up a business card, take out an advertisement, or distribute a flyer with the word "counselor" and a list of services he or she is willing to provide. Some of these self-anointed counselors may try to impress their clientele with mail-order degrees, but they have no legitimate training in evaluating and treating mental health problems.

Who Guards the Guardians?

Who makes sure that physicians practice good medicine? Right now, there are few effective guardians. Most quality assurance efforts are aimed at weeding out only those physicians who are grossly incompetent or at creating incentives for physicians to learn new information. Hospitals monitor the inpatient performance of their affiliated physicians; all federally qualified HMOs and the larger fee-for-service group practices regularly evaluate performance.

On the whole, the medical profession has merely paid lip service to the need to rid its ranks of the seriously incompetent. If a physician is an alcohol or drug abuser, or too old or infirm to perform surgery, colleagues may decide to report him or her to a hospital disciplinary board, local medical society, or state licensing board. Or they may not.

To encourage physicians to stay abreast of new knowledge, most states now require them to obtain a certain number of hours of continuing education before they can renew their licenses, but that requirement guarantees only that doctors attend lectures or listen to taped instruction; it does not ensure that they learn anything or that they use new information in their medical practices.

Most medical specialties now require that physicians take examinations every seven to ten years to demonstrate their continuing mastery. Specialists in both family medicine and pediatrics who wish to remain board-certified must pass an exam every seven years. Internists have a voluntary recertification program that became mandatory in 1990; now, internists who become board-certified or recertified must go through an extensive evaluation process, including a written examination, every ten years to remain board-certified.

Accountability may become far more common as business, government, and consumers of health care demand greater oversight of the medical profession. According to Dennis O'Leary, M.D., President of the Joint Commission on Accreditation of Healthcare Organizations, "pressure is building for the development of quality assurance programs that would evaluate fee-for-service practice."[28] At the end of 1989, the federal government began a new pilot program to study the quality of care being provided to Medicare beneficiaries in physicians' offices. Under the aegis of the Wisconsin Peer Review Organization, care will be reviewed in the offices of selected physicians in seven states: Wisconsin, Arizona, Connecticut, Indiana, North Carolina, Utah, and Washington. On the state level, New York may become the first to require periodic reviews of physicians for competence; other states are considering similar systems for the future.

4

How Financial Incentives May Influence Doctors' Decisions

Physicians are human beings. Some are highly ethical practitioners selflessly devoted to their patients and to the science of medicine. Some are self-serving money-makers who see their patients more as income-producing units than as individuals. And in between are the majority of doctors, who are more or less affected by the kinds of forces that affect us all. Thus, financial incentives are likely to influence the behavior of members of the medical profession, and the payment mechanisms of a given type of insurance plan may well affect an individual physician's behavior.

In 1911, George Bernard Shaw, turning his sharp gaze on the financial motives of the medical profession, pointed out:

> That any sane nation, having observed that you could provide for the supply of bread by giving bakers a pecuniary interest in baking for you, should go on to give a surgeon a pecuniary interest in cutting off your leg, is enough to make one despair of political humanity. But that is precisely what we have done. And the more appalling the mutilation, the more the mutilator is paid.[1]

Even though medical care improved tremendously during, and beyond, Shaw's long lifetime, his lesson in perverse incentives remains true in our age of medical wonders. And now, eighty years later, health planners and economists are paying increasing attention to *the way* the people who provide health care make money, not just *how much* money they make, and they are showing us the relationship between the seemingly uncontrollable increase in our country's health care costs and its reimbursement system.

How Physicians Are Paid

There are three ways that American physicians are paid for the care they provide patients: fee-for-service, fee-for-time, and fee-per-patient. In addition to these basic payment methods, physicians may have bonuses or profit-sharing plans.

Fee-for-service. This is the payment method most familiar to patients in the United States. Fee-for-service physicians are paid for each service they provide either by the patient, the insurance company, or the government (e.g., Medicare or Medicaid). The physician may be either self-employed or may be an employee or owner of a physician-owned organization (group practice). Most American physicians prefer fee-for-service practice.

Fee-for-time. Physicians paid this way may receive a salary from an organization. A physician who is not a full-time employee of the organization may be paid on an hourly, or retainer, basis. Under any of these terms, the physician agrees to work a certain number of hours per week in exchange for a given amount of money. The earnings of such physicians are not affected by how many patients they see, how many procedures they do, or how many tests they order. This is the most common way of paying physicians who work for group practice HMOs, medical schools, and teaching hospitals.

Fee-per-patient. This method is called capitation (the physician is paid *per capita*). It is one component of the payment method used by the British national health system to reimburse general practitioners; the more patients in their "panel," the greater the payment from the government. In this country, it is used primarily by HMOs that do not pay salaries to physicians but instead negotiate a monthly or annual payment for each member who signs up with a given physician or group of physicians. The doctors receive this set capitation payment (which commonly varies by age and sex) regardless of the amount of medical services their HMO patients use.

Financial Incentives in Fee-for-Service Practice

Although this arrangement seems familiar and straightforward to most people, it is often attacked by health planners and economists, as well as by a number of physicians, who have identified its expense and potential dangers. Simply stated, because physicians are rewarded directly for "doing," they may tend to do too much. Patients may make unnecessary office visits, have extra tests, and, of most concern, undergo unnecessary procedures.

According to Arnold Relman, M.D., editor of *The New England Journal of Medicine:*

> The fee-for-service arrangement, even when softened by charity, has always had an obvious and inherent conflict of interest for the physician. In economic terms, the fee-for-service physician is a supplier who is able to determine the demand for his own services. By virtue of his special knowledge, the authority vested in him by the state, and the trusting consent of his patient, the fee-for-service physician makes the decision to use the medical services that he himself provides, and for which he will be paid on a piecework basis. It is a situation with a built-in potential for abuse.[2]

Ethical doctors make decisions based on the needs of their patients, but there are powerful forces that intensify the conflicts of interest inherent in fee-for-service practice:

- the desire of physicians to avoid malpractice suits by ordering extra tests and procedures
- insurance reimbursement schedules that pay physicians much more for doing procedures than for using cognitive skills to counsel, discuss treatment alternatives, and educate patients
- requests by patients for the doctor to "do something," often by utilizing the latest and most expensive technology, even if watchful waiting might be a better alternative

Physicians who are, or will be, in the position to purchase supplies and equipment are prime targets for drug companies and manufacturers of these items. An article in *The New England Journal of Medicine* described a medical conference for gastroenterologists, sponsored by a manufacturer of laboratory equipment. Directors of training programs were invited to select one Fellow (senior trainee) to send. "The conference was to take place at a posh resort in Florida, and expenses for air transportation, lodging, food, golf and tennis would be provided for each Fellow."[3] And the next year, if that physician opens a practice, which company would likely come to mind when he or she is buying equipment?

Conflicts of Interest

Laboratories. Some physicians own an interest in a laboratory to which they send their own patients. Although New York City has made it illegal for a physician to bill patients for tests done in a laboratory that he or she owns, most communities have no such law. In mid-1989, the Inspector General of the Department of Health and Human Services released a report that found that 12 percent of physicians who treat Medicare patients refer them to laboratories and other facilities in which they have financial interests. Patients of these physicians received 45 percent more clinical laboratory services than all Medicare patients in general, and 13 percent more specialized radiological tests.

On January 1, 1992, a federal law will go into effect that prohibits physicians with ownership interests in clinical laboratories from referring Medicare patients to those labs. Exceptions will be made for physicians who own stock in a clinical laboratory that is large enough to be listed on the New York or American stock exchange, and has assets of more than $100 million. Clinical labs in physicians' offices are also excepted, as are labs maintained by hospitals and HMOs and those owned by rural providers. Exceptions will also be made for physicians who own shares of facilities that house imaging equipment, such as magnetic resonance imagers or computerized tomographic scanners, as well as X-ray equipment.

Medical equipment. Dr. Relman and other writers on the topic of medical ethics are troubled about possible conflicts of interest for physicians who own shares in companies that manufacture medical equipment. But there is an even greater conflict of interest for physicians who own the equipment itself, especially if it is highly specialized and very expensive. An expensive new piece of equipment must be paid for. Thus, there may be an incentive to overuse it.

Specialized office equipment is advertised aggressively, with direct mailings that show physicians how quickly they can pay back the cost of purchase by doing tests frequently. According to an advertisement for a piece of diagnostic equipment that costs $4,995, the test "takes five minutes" and is "easy to administer and interpret." The copy goes on to state that the average Medicare reimbursement for the test is $125—up to $250 in southern Florida.[4]

Some of the technologically advanced equipment is so expensive that no one physician can afford to buy it. For example, a computerized tomographic scanner sells for more than a million dollars, and a magnetic resonance imager can cost between three and four million dollars. To purchase one, a consortium of physicians may be assembled that includes not only those who will use the equipment directly but also physicians who are most likely to refer patients to the testing facility. Membership in such a consortium creates a far greater potential conflict of interest than ownership of stock in a publicly traded company, and it should be fully disclosed to the patient, although this has seldom been the practice.

Drugs. Drug companies used to put all their efforts into encouraging physicians to write prescriptions for a particular drug; now they encourage physicians to buy drugs to sell directly to their patients. Physicians who sell drugs commonly add a "filling fee" to the cost of the drug, even though they are merely handing the patient a prepackaged, prelabeled vial. The Office of the Inspector General of the Department of Health and Human Services has drafted a report recommending that doctors who dispense drugs be required to register with the state and to provide patients with information about the cost of the drug, so that they can make an informed choice about where to purchase it.[5]

Hospitals. Physicians who invest in hospital corporations in their own communities have a built-in conflict of interest. They may be reluctant to send patients to a rival hospital even if it offers better services. To further complicate matters, some hospitals have begun to buy physicians' practices for substantial sums of money, with the provision that the physician make all future referrals to the hospital that owns the practice. Patients are usually unaware of this ownership relationship between hospitals and physicians' practices, and it is not in their best interest.

Incentives in Small-Scale Practice and Group Practice

For many years, small-scale fee-for-service practices were the norm in this country, and they are still typical in smaller communities and in New York City. The financial incentives could not be simpler: the more physicians do, the more they earn.

Primary care physicians in this setting make most of their money from fees for office visits, supplemented by fees for visits to hospitalized patients and for simple office procedures such as a urinalysis or an electrocardiogram. Specialists can charge higher fees for office visits and provide more extensive services depending on their field of expertise. They may offer X rays, sigmoidoscopy, colonoscopy, or even minor surgery in their offices. Physicians in a number of surgical specialties make most of their money from doing procedures in the hospital and use their offices primarily for consultations and for follow-up visits after surgery.

Increasingly, however, physicians are practicing in groups. These may be either "single-specialty" groups, with all the physicians practicing the same specialty, or "multispecialty" groups, in which physicians with a number of different specialties join forces.

Single-specialty groups are usually small—fewer than ten physicians—and their incentives are similar to those of a one- or two-person practice. The two main reasons for physicians to form a single-specialty group are to share the overhead of equipping and maintaining a practice and to share the burden of taking care of patients after office hours or when one physician is away on vacation. A group is more apt to own a lab and invest more heavily in specialized equipment than would a solo practitioner.

Multispecialty groups, however, are substantially different from solo practices and from most single-specialty groups. They are often much larger (from twenty-five physicians up to several hundred in the largest groups), and they are organized to serve different purposes. A large multispecialty group practice is a medical business jointly owned by physician-partners.

One of the key goals of such a practice is to provide "one-stop shopping" to its patients. Therefore, it will attempt to hire physicians in most specialties, make extensive purchases of medical equipment, set up well-equipped laboratories, and develop its own physical therapy and laboratory departments.

It will offer centralized medical records, on-the-spot referrals to specialists, and convenient arrangements for diagnostic or screening tests.

Many features of a multispecialty group are consistent with the interests of patients: convenience, easy access to ancillary services, and a centralized medical record. The largest group practices—the Mayo Clinic, the Cleveland Clinic, the Ochsner Clinic, the Virginia Mason Clinic—own their own hospitals, and this may further enhance coordinated care and convenience.

But the usual fee-for-service incentives to "do more" may be magnified in a group practice setting, depending on how physicians are paid. A few practices pay salaries to most members of their staff, and a few pay exclusively on the basis of each physician's "production" (the revenue the physician generates for the group). Most large group practices have more complex compensation systems.

Most groups treat new physicians as employees and include them as partners after determining whether the newcomer meets the group's standards. The physician-partner's earnings are then based on a combination of three factors:

- a salary, or "draw," that varies by specialty
- a percentage of his or her production
- a percentage of the group's profits for the year

The physician's production is calculated by adding up his or her "billings" for the year; that is, how much fee-for-service revenue was generated in visits and procedures. Most fee-for-service group practices pay bonuses based on the production of the individual physician. Some group practices include in their calculation of production the dollar value of laboratory tests, X rays, and electrocardiograms. And, since performing more tests increases the group's revenues, there may be peer pressure on the individual physician to do diagnostic and screening tests whenever possible, since the whole group benefits from this approach.

Physicians practicing in multispecialty groups also have an incentive to make referrals to their colleagues; the more referrals, the greater the group's revenues. Thus, there is the potential for unnecessary referrals within the group or referrals based not on the absolute qualifications of the specialist but on his or her membership in the group practice. Although it is considered unethical for a physician in solo practice to benefit financially from making referrals (the practice is called "fee-splitting"), physicians in group practice who routinely share in group profits are not considered unethical.

How You Can Protect Yourself from Unnecessary Medical Care

Doctors in fee-for-service practice generate more income by seeing patients more often. They may recommend screening tests and routine visits more frequently than is medically necessary. These are some behaviors that are rewarded by fee-for-service financial incentives:

- instructing parents to come in for well-baby visits once a month for the first year
- seeing patients on medication for high blood pressure once a month
- telling office receptionists to squeeze in all patients who request appointments
- ordering screening laboratory tests (if they have their own laboratory equipment)
- doing surgical procedures, such as removing gallbladders, uteruses, prostates

If you sign up for an indemnity policy or preferred provider insurance, you will choose doctors who work in fee-for-service settings. To counteract fee-for-service incentives to do more than is necessary, you can ask the kinds of questions we have suggested about tests, drugs, and surgery, and you can try to choose a doctor that impresses you with his or her professional integrity. (See chapter 3, pages 87–90 for a list of questions to ask your doctor.)

If you wonder whether a doctor's visit is necessary, explore alternatives. You may be able to save money and time. If you have a chronic condition, your doctor may be able to instruct you in self-care or find ways to reduce your costs for office visits. For example, if you need frequent blood pressure checks, your doctor may be able to teach you to monitor your blood pressure at home or may arrange to have the office nurse check your pressure for a small fee. In this way, you would need to see the physician only if a problem arose.

If you want screening or routine visits on a less frequent basis, you can ask the physician if public health experts differ on how often a particular kind of care is needed. For example, parents of healthy infants may find monthly visits helpful if they are anxious about their baby's health or if their physician is particularly interested in child development and is able to spend time answering questions and discussing problems. But monthly visits in the first year are not necessary unless the baby has a medical problem. Parents who ask will learn that many experts think that less frequent visits are sufficient and that normal babies need to be seen two weeks after birth and then at two, four, six, nine, and twelve months.

If, at the end of an appointment, your doctor suggests that you schedule a follow-up visit after a week or two of treatment, ask whether you will need to be seen if you no longer have symptoms. In many cases, a follow-up visit may be unnecessary for someone who is feeling well.

Financial Incentives in HMO Practice

Health maintenance organizations are paid in advance to take care of their members, and this fact creates a very different set of financial incentives for HMO physicians. A prepaid plan makes a deal with its members, which can be reduced to the following simple statement: give us a specified amount of money up front, and we will be responsible for providing or paying for whatever medical care you need.

At first glance, withholding care may appear to be a fundamental financial strategy of an HMO. The less it spends on its members' needs, the more it gets to keep. In reality, the financial incentives of a prepaid plan are more complex and operate as a system of checks and balances. It is in the financial interest of an HMO to provide each patient with exactly the right amount of care. Providing unnecessary care costs money, and plans that fail to limit unnecessary care are bound to go out of business. But withholding necessary care also has its cost to HMOs because it contributes to a sicker and more expensive patient population. A plan that deliberately withheld necessary care as a financial strategy would also risk lawsuits, bad publicity, loss of members, and ultimately business failure.

How Group Practice HMOs Reward Physicians

While HMOs all operate with the same basic financial incentives, the specific ways in which HMO physicians are rewarded will vary. You will need to know a few more details about how different types of HMOs are organized in order to understand differences in the ways they compensate their physicians.

In other chapters, we have included both staff model and group model HMOs under the heading "group practice plans." In most cases, distinctions between them are irrelevant to members except when it comes to considering financial incentives.

Staff model HMOs. This type of HMO hires full-time physicians and pays them salaries based primarily on their specialties and seniority. The organization commonly develops standards for how many patients physicians are expected to see in a week, and it monitors the physicians' use of medical resources, such as the number and/or expense of referrals each makes.

In staff model HMOs, physicians have no direct financial incentive to provide or deny care to a specific patient; however, the organization as a whole benefits if, overall, there are fewer visits and procedures. If a staff model HMO is having difficulty controlling costs, there may be organizational pressure on physicians to lower their utilization of medical services.

Group model HMOs. Here, physicians form a partnership and contract with the HMO to provide care to a defined group of members. The partnership is paid a set sum of money each year, based on an average amount per patient. This "capitation" fee is derived through actuarial analysis.

The physician group then takes over all responsibility for providing medical care for HMO members. If the physicians can provide this care for less than the capitation amount paid by the HMO, they will have money left over at the end of the year; if they are less efficient, they will make less money than they initially projected.

In the largest group model plans, the physician group is fully or partly responsible for the costs of caring for HMO members in the hospital; in the smaller plans, only a small portion of the hospital costs are the financial responsibility of the physicians.

Bonuses. Many staff and group model HMOs pay bonuses to physicians. The amount usually represents a fairly small percentage of the physician's total salary, commonly under 10 percent. Most plans that have bonus programs base their bonuses on a combination of two factors: how profitable the plan is as a whole and how well costs are controlled by defined subgroups of physicians (all the doctors in a certain region or in a given health care center). Only a very small percentage of group practice model HMOs base their bonus programs on how well an individual physician's referrals to outside specialists were controlled.

Physicians in both staff and group model HMOs have the following financial incentives:

- providing the fewest visits that are compatible with effective medical care
- ordering only those screening tests that are proven to be useful
- referring patients for consultations only when the physician believes they are medically necessary
- admitting patients to the hospital only when there is no medically safe alternative

How IPAs Reward Physicians

If you sign up with an HMO and choose a primary care physician from its list of practitioners in the community, you have chosen either an IPA (Independent Practice Association) model HMO or a PCN (Primary Care Network) HMO. In an IPA, the HMO contracts with an association of fee-for-service physicians who wish to see HMO members. In a PCN, the HMO contracts directly with individual fee-for-service primary care doctors (or small groups). Physicians may be paid in one of two ways.

Discounted fee-for-service. IPAs that pay physicians on this basis first negotiate a discount from the physician's regular fee and may then withhold some of the discounted fee in an escrow fund to cover the HMO's risk of experiencing high medical costs. At the end of the year, if expenses are lower than expected, a portion of the fund is distributed to participating physicians according to a predetermined formula.

But physicians who are paid on a discounted fee-for-service basis continue to have fee-for-service financial incentives. Discounts do not really affect these incentives because the physician still stands to make more money by providing more medical care.

Even though the HMO monitors the frequency of visits, referral patterns, and lengths of hospitalizations—and occasionally terminates a physician who consistently utilizes resources extravagantly—it will generally be unable to control costs effectively, and the withheld fee is seldom paid.

Capitation. In order to control costs, IPA HMOs are increasingly turning to capitation. Physicians who are paid on a capitation basis have no financial incentive to see HMO patients more than necessary. If anything, there is a risk that they will give preference to their fee-for-service patients, whose extra visits would lead to more revenue.

This risk, however, is balanced by the ability of HMO members to change physicians if they are not satisfied. A physician who is not responsive to HMO members' needs will lose patients—and the capitation fee that comes with them.

As in discounted fee-for-service plans, many plans that use capitation withhold a portion of the primary care physician's payment and return it at the end of the year if expenses are on budget.

Financial incentives that put the patient at risk. Most IPAs and PCNs use a "gatekeeper" approach to cost control by requiring their members to receive prior approval for almost all services from a primary care physician—the "gatekeeper." Most plans also limit the financial risk to be borne by their primary care physicians to those costs that the doctors can control themselves. And the physicians' incentives to withhold care are balanced by their desire to retain patients.

A handful of plans, however, have gone far beyond rewarding physicians for their success in controlling primary care costs. These plans create separate accounts for their physicians and credit these accounts with funds to cover *all* of the medical expenses of the HMO members they each serve. In this situation, each time your primary care doctor sends you to a lab, refers you to a specialist, or admits you to the hospital, the HMO pays the bill against your physician's own account.

At the end of the year the HMO audits the accounts. Those physicians who show a surplus for the year receive a bonus—usually 30 to 50 percent of the total surplus in the account. Those who show a deficit must forfeit part of the monthly capitation they have received during the past year—sometimes as much as 25 percent.[6] Physicians in this situation may be tempted to withhold necessary care from their patients to protect themselves from financial risk.

Even though this payment method appears to resemble that found in capitated group model HMOs, there are substantial differences. Group model plans may employ fifty to five hundred doctors. They can afford to hire a number of specialists, thereby reducing referral costs significantly. And they can spread their financial risk over a large number of physicians.

The actuarial method used to calculate capitation payments is designed to work on a large scale, and it is useful in estimating the costs of providing care to tens of thousands of patients. However, it is a very unreliable way of forecasting costs on a small scale to determine payments to a single physician who is responsible only for several hundred patients.

For example, an account might be credited with $8,000 per month to cover the costs of referral to specialists and hospital care for two hundred HMO patients. Most months the doctor would do well. But if just one patient should need heart surgery, the costs might easily reach $25,000. If other patients should need specialty or hospital care during the next few months, the physician would be in debt to the HMO. The financial incentives to withhold care in this setup are obvious, and risky for patients.

In 1988 the General Accounting Office (GAO) of the federal government made some recommendations concerning physician incentives in HMOs. The GAO believes that the more the HMO transfers financial risks to physicians and the more closely incentives are linked to decisions about individual patients, the greater the potential threat to quality of care. Legislation is being considered that would prohibit HMOs from making direct payments to a physician as an inducement to withhold or limit necessary services to an identifiable patient.

Fortunately, IPA model HMOs are now moving away from using incentives that put physicians at too much financial risk. In doing so, they have been spurred on by a desire to avoid the adverse publicity they received when the GAO and others criticized these programs—and by a fear of litigation. Several HMO members who belonged to plans with "risky" financial incentives have sued, claiming that the HMO's incentives contributed to the physicians' decisions to withhold care.

Making Sure You Get Necessary Care

Just as there are questions you can ask to protect yourself against the risk of unnecessary care, there are also those you can ask if you are concerned that the incentives of a particular plan favor withholding care.

You might begin by calling the HMO administrative office to find out how the plan pays its physicians. In a group practice plan, bonuses, if any, should be only partially related to the success of a given physician in containing costs. In an IPA that pays by capitation, no more than 15 percent of a physician's earnings should be based on his or her success in controlling costs.

If you think you need a test, visit, or referral and your HMO physician disagrees, find out the basis for his or her disagreement. Ask about the risks of a particular test or treatment, and if those risks seem minimal to you compared to the benefits, ask the doctor why he or she is not willing to order the treatment you feel you need. If you have visited a primary care physician for the same problem several times, and you are not satisfied with the care you are receiving, urge the doctor to refer you to a specialist, and ask for an explanation of any refusal to do so.

How Financial Incentives May Affect Your Choice of Health Insurance

No system of financial incentives is perfect. There are problems inherent in both fee-for-service practice and in prepaid health plans. By staying alert to the ways in which these incentives can affect your health care, you can protect yourself from those conflicts of interest that concern you the most.

If your deepest concern is the possibility that you may be

denied necessary care, you will lean toward purchasing indemnity or preferred provider insurance. If, on the other hand, you fear the possibility of being subjected to the dangers of unnecessary tests and surgery, you will prefer a prepaid health plan. Although there is no way to guarantee that a fee-for-service doctor will never omit a necessary test or that an HMO will always spare you unnecessary medical care, you can at least choose the type of insurance plan that seems most congruent with your own particular concerns and, by doing so, avoid the constant conflict that would arise if you did not agree with the underlying incentives of a given system.

5

How to Compare Health Insurance Plans

How do you compare an indemnity health plan, a PPO, and an HMO? If your employer offers five different plans for your consideration, how do you go about comparing the benefits? (Some employers, including the federal government and many state governments, may offer six, ten, or even more choices.) If you are confused by the array of possibilities offered, you may be tempted to sign up for the same plan you have always used. Resist the temptation. You may be able to turn confusion into opportunity by discovering that another health insurance plan is more comprehensive, less expensive, or better suited to your particular needs. To do so, you must make some careful assessments of the *value* of each plan, and that value includes more than its apparent cost on paper.

In addition to evaluating the financial worth to you of a given plan, you need to consider how well the plan suits your own situation and preferences. Do you have a long-standing relationship with a trusted physician or are you looking for a new doctor? Do you want to make all your own medical choices or would you prefer to have arrangements made for you?

Take an honest look at your behavior. If you are careless about keeping records and filing forms, your habits will likely detract from the value of an indemnity policy that looked like a reasonable deal on paper.

If you are annoyed by rules and systems, you may feel constrained by the restrictions of an HMO or a PPO. If you ignore them, however, you will cost yourself money you hadn't planned to spend. Your employer will give you the opportunity to change plans only once a year. The more carefully you choose the kind of insurance and the specific plan you prefer, the less likely you are to regret the decision you make.

Cost Comparisons

Finding out what each plan is worth to you is a fairly straightforward first step; comparing the value of several plans of the same type is somewhat trickier. Now you are about to compare indemnity plans, PPOs, and HMOs. To do this, you will need a more sophisticated method of analysis than the one you would use to compare one indemnity plan with another or one HMO with another. This method will work whether you buy your own policy or sign up for a group plan at work.

Comparing Three Types of Plans

Let's assume that your employer has just given you the following three options.

A typical indemnity plan. Mutual Providential of Hartford is an indemnity health insurance plan with a $100 individual/ $300 family deductible, 80 percent co-insurance, a stop-loss of $3,000, and no coverage for preventive services (pap smears, mammograms, blood pressure checks) or wellness care (well-child exams, periodic adult exams, immunizations). Your employer pays the premium in full for employees. For families, the plan costs $255 a month, of which the employer pays $205, leaving you with a monthly contribution to the premium of $50. Prescription drugs are covered at 80 percent, once the basic deductible is satisfied.

A typical PPO. Preferred Choiceplan, a PPO, pays 90 percent of covered expenses, and there is no deductible if you use only preferred providers, with the exception of hospital emergency room visits, which are subject to a $25 deductible. If you do not use providers from the plan's preferred list, you must pay a $100 deductible, and the plan will then cover only 70 percent of your costs above the deductible. There is no coverage for preventive and wellness care. Members are charged $3 for each prescription at specified pharmacies. The plan has a stop-loss of $3,000. Your employer pays the entire premium for your own coverage, but you are required to pay $50 a month toward the premium cost if you want to cover your family.

A typical HMO. Community Health Plan is an HMO that features comprehensive coverage. It requires co-payments of $3 per office visit, $3 per prescription, and $25 per emergency room visit; your own premium is fully paid by your employer. Your employer pays $205 toward the family premium of $275; if you want to cover your family, your contribution to the premium is $70 a month. (This is $20 more per month, or $240 more per year, than either the straight indemnity or the PPO plan.)

Which plan is a better financial deal? The HMO will cost you $240 more per year in premium payments for family coverage. Both the indemnity plan and the PPO have reasonable stop-loss figures of $3,000, thereby offering catastrophic coverage almost as good as that provided by the HMO. If you and your family needed no health care in the next year, you would save $240 by signing up with the indemnity plan or the PPO; both would be better deals than the HMO. But if, like most people, you need some health care each year, you must look beyond the $240 difference in premium cost when comparing the three different plans and try to assess what the coverage you are buying will be worth to you when you actually have to use it. How much will your policy pay toward your medical expenses, and how much will you pay out of your own pocket?

Target Areas

One fairly simple way to do a comparison is to list all your medical bills for the past two years and see to what extent each plan would have covered them. But if those two years are not typical of what you expect your future expenses to be, you can, instead, look at how each plan would cover four target areas: routine care (including prevention and wellness care), minor episodic care, prescription drugs, and hospitalization or other major expense. The target-area method will work for people with simple or complex medical needs, and it can be used to compare any of the health insurance policies you are considering.

In the examples that follow, we'll look at the medical needs of a single woman in her thirties and those of a family of four. We will assume that none of these people has any unusual medical problem. The health insurance policies they are comparing are typical of those that many employers offer. We have assumed here that the family in our examples is covered by a single policy. (For information on dual coverage, see pages 147–50.)

To keep the computations simple, we have rounded off the numbers and we have assumed, when calculating costs for the indemnity plan, that physicians' fees fall within its definition of what is usual, customary, and reasonable (UCR). If the physicians you use charge fees in excess of UCR, remember that you will be responsible for *all* of that excess amount. Furthermore, charges above the UCR level cannot be applied to satisfy a deductible or a stop-loss. If, for instance, your doctor charges you $150 and your policy allows a UCR maximum of $100, you must consider the additional $50 as your own out-of-pocket expense. (See chapter 1 for a full discussion of UCR and fee schedules.)

Target area one: routine care. Most people have personal patterns of routine care (medical visits for no identified illness or medical problem). In general, men under age forty are comparatively low users of all types of medical care; they may have periodic routine physical exams, but many do not seek any type of routine care. Most women have one or two routine exams a year. Infants usually have six to eight routine exams the first year of life, and two to four the next; older children have one or two a year. In the example that follows, we assume the family of four is conscientious about screening and prevention; the children, taken together, make three routine visits, the mother, two, and the father, one.

A national survey published in *Medical Economics* (October 2, 1989) found that, on the average, an internist charged $90 to $135 for a complete history and physical; a gynecologist charged $30 to $40 for a checkup and $10 to $15 for a pap smear; and a pediatrician charged $30 to $35 for a checkup and $20 to $35 for an immunization. Thus, in 1990, a family of four could expect to spend somewhere between $200 and $400 in physicians' fees for this level of care. None of their expenses would be covered by the indemnity plan or the PPO; the HMO, however, would cover all of this care, with a copayment of $3 for each visit. The following examples show how the three different types of insurance cover routine care.

SINGLE WOMAN

Mutual Providential (Indemnity)

Number of visits	Cost per visit	Cost for year
2	$50	$100

Preferred Choiceplan (PPO)

Number of visits	Cost per visit	Cost for year
2	$50	$100

Community Health Plan (HMO)

Number of visits	Co-payment per visit	Cost for year
2	$3	$6

Under the indemnity plan and the PPO, the single woman would pay $100 out of pocket per year, since neither plan provides coverage for routine care. Under the HMO plan, her out-of-pocket expense would be $6 in co-payments.

FAMILY OF FOUR

Mutual Providential (Indemnity)

	Number of visits	Cost per visit		Cost for year
Father	1	$125		$125
Mother	2	50		100
10-year-old	1	40		40
3-year-old	2	40		80
			Total:	$345

Preferred Choiceplan (PPO)

	Number of visits	Cost per visit		Cost for year
Father	1	$125		$125
Mother	2	50		100
10-year-old	1	40		40
3-year-old	2	40		80
			Total:	$345

Community Health Plan (HMO)

	Number of visits	Cost per visit		Cost for year
Father	1	$3		$ 3
Mother	2	3		6
10-year-old	1	3		3
3-year-old	2	3		6
			Total:	$18

Neither the indemnity plan nor the PPO covers routine care; the family of four would pay all costs themselves, and their total out-of-pocket expense would be $345. Under the HMO plan, the $3 co-payment charges for six visits would add up to a total out-of-pocket expense of $18 for the year.

Target area two: minor episodic care. This category includes lacerations, sprains that need to be X-rayed, ear infections, rashes, vaginitis, flu that you thought was bronchitis, and the like. Most families have a few minor medical problems each year, perhaps one per person per year. Our example assumes one medical problem for the single woman and five for the family of four, one of which involved an emergency room visit. An indemnity health insurance plan will require that you satisfy a deductible first. An HMO will not, but it will probably charge small co-payments for each of these visits, or a larger co-payment if care is given in a hospital emergency room. Most PPOs don't require you to satisfy a deductible if you use preferred providers.

Let's assume that this woman's first medical problem of the year is a sinus infection. How would she fare under each of the three different plans?

SINGLE WOMAN

Mutual Providential (Indemnity)

Problem	Fee
Sinus infection	$120
Cost to patient ($100 deductible plus 20% of $20)	104

Preferred Choice Plan (PPO)

Problem	Fee
Sinus infection	$120
Cost to patient (10% co-insurance)	12

Community Healthplan (HMO)

Problem	Co-payment
Sinus infection	$3
Cost to patient	3

The indemnity plan has a $100 deductible, so most of this first medical bill will not be reimbursed. To calculate how much her insurance policy will pay, the woman subtracts the $100 deductible from her $120 medical bill; the $20 balance above the deductible level will be reimbursed by Mutual Providential at 80 percent of allowable charges, or $16. She must pay $4 in co-insurance. To calculate her total out-of-pocket expense, she adds the $100 deductible, for which she is responsible, to the $4 she paid toward the physician's fee. Her total out-of-pocket expense is $104.

There is no deductible with Preferred Choiceplan. Assuming she chooses a physician from the plan's preferred list, she will pay only 10 percent of the total charge of $120, or $12. In the HMO plan, she would pay only the $3 co-payment.

FAMILY OF FOUR

Mutual Providential (Indemnity)

	Problem		Fee
Father	Minor laceration		$ 90
Mother	Sinus infection		120
10-year-old	Flu		35
3-year-old	Ear infection		40
	Atopic dermatitis		40
		Total:	$325
	Cost to family ($300 deductible plus 20% of $25):		305

Preferred Choiceplan (PPO)

	Problem		Charges
Father	Minor laceration		$ 90
Mother	Sinus infection		120
10-year-old	Flu		35
3-year-old	Ear infection		40
	Atopic dermatitis		40
		Total:	$325
	Cost to family ($25 ER deductible plus 10% co-insurance):		55

Community Health Plan (HMO)

	Problem	Co-payment
Father	Minor laceration	$25
Mother	Sinus infection	3
10-year-old	Flu	3
3-year-old	Ear infection	3
	Atopic dermatitis	3
	Total:	$37
	Cost to family:	37

Under the indemnity policy, the family of four must first satisfy the $300 family deductible before any of their medical bills become eligible for reimbursement. Only $25 of their bills for minor episodic care would be covered at 80 percent co-insurance. Mutual Providential pays $20 and they pay the remaining $5. Their total out-of-pocket expense would be the $300 deductible plus $5, or $305. However, once the deductible has been satisfied, future bills will be covered at 80 percent.

Under the PPO plan, there is no overall deductible to satisfy so long as preferred providers are used, but the plan has a $25 deductible for emergency room visits. Because the father's minor laceration was treated in a hospital emergency room, the family had to pay the $25 deductible, plus 10 percent of the remaining $300, for a total out-of-pocket expense of $55.

Under the HMO, there is no deductible and no co-insurance, but there are co-payments of $3 for office visits. Since the father was referred by the HMO to the emergency room of one of its designated hospitals for repair of his laceration, he had to pay a $25 ER co-payment. The total out-of-pocket expense for minor episodic care for the family of four would be $37.

Target area three: prescription drugs. If you take drugs for chronic problems, you can project your medication costs for the year. The kinds of minor, episodic medical problems we described in the preceding examples are also apt to lead to a few prescriptions. The average cost of such a prescription is somewhere between $15 and $20. How would a single person and a family fare under our three different insurance plans?

A majority of indemnity plans require that subscribers first satisfy a deductible before prescription drug expenses are covered at the co-insurance rate. Some indemnity policies are coupled with a separate plan that covers drugs for a co-payment, with no requirement for a deductible to be satisfied. Most HMOs and PPOs charge a small co-payment for drugs, with no requirement that a deductible be satisfied.

With Mutual Providential's indemnity plan, prescriptions are covered at 80 percent after the deductible is met. The single woman satisfied her deductible with the physician's bill for treating the sinus infection. Assuming her prescription cost is $15, her drug expense would be $3 (20% of $15). The HMO and the PPO charge a $3 co-payment for all prescription drugs (regardless of what the drug costs). Under this scenario, the single woman's out-of-pocket expense for drugs with all three plans would be $3.

For the family of four, medications to treat sinusitis, an ear infection, and atopic dermatitis would come to about $50. Under the indemnity plan, the family's co-insurance share would be 20 percent of that cost, or $10, since they had met their family deductible. With the HMO or the PPO, the total would be $9 in co-payments for the three prescriptions.

Comparing coverage for ordinary medical expenses. Before we move on to target area four—major expenses and hospitalization—it would be useful to compare the total annual out-of-pocket expense for ordinary care that the single woman and family of four would incur under the three policies we have been considering.

SINGLE WOMAN

Comparison of Annual Out-of-Pocket Expenses

	Mutual Providential (Indemnity)	Preferred Choiceplan (PPO)	Community Healthplan (HMO)
Premium contribution	$0	$0	$0
Routine care	100	100	6
Minor episodic care	104	12	3
Prescriptions	3	3	3
Total for year	$207	$115	$12

Although the single woman has no expense in premium contribution, her out-of-pocket costs under each of the three insurance plans are quite different. It will cost her $195 more per year if she chooses the indemnity plan instead of the HMO, and $103 more per year if she selects the PPO rather than the HMO.

FAMILY OF FOUR

Comparison of Annual Out-of-Pocket Expenses

	Mutual Providential (Indemnity)	Preferred Choiceplan (PPO)	Community Healthplan (HMO)
Premium contribution	$600	$600	$840
Routine care	345	345	18
Minor episodic care	305	55	37
Prescriptions	10	9	9
Total for year	$1,260	$1,009	$904

Again, premium costs alone are not a reliable guide to the comparative worth of a particular plan. Although the HMO costs $240 more per year in premiums than the indemnity plan or the PPO, joining it would actually save this family $356 per year compared with the indemnity plan and $105 per year compared with the PPO.

Target area four: major expenses and hospitalization. So far, we've been comparing the costs of minor problems. But to test the financial worth of a health insurance policy, you must estimate how well it would cover you for the more common kinds of expensive medical care such as obstetrics or elective surgery as well as for unforeseen catastrophic expenses.

If you are planning a pregnancy, or if you have decided to have elective surgery, you already know you are going to use your insurance.

How would these three plans work for you if you and your spouse have decided to start a family? You learn that fee-for-service obstetricians in your community charge about $1,500 for prenatal care and a routine delivery, and you find out that a hospital stay will cost $1,000 if you limit it to one day after delivery. Which policy would offer the best financial coverage?

Indemnity. Mutual Providential would pay 80 percent of your physician's fees, once you have satisfied the deductible for the year. Assuming that you had not, your cost would be the $100 deductible plus your 20 percent share of the obstetrical and hospital costs: $280 and $200 respectively. Total out-of-pocket expense = $580.

PPO. Preferred Choiceplan has no deductible if you use only preferred providers, and the plan pays 90 percent of the obstetrician and hospital cost. Total out-of-pocket expense = $250.

HMO. The only fees Community Healthplan charges are $3 co-payments for office visits. Hospital expenses would be fully covered. For an average pregnancy, you could expect eleven prenatal visits. Total out-of-pocket expense = $33.

How would these three plans work for you if you needed surgery? Suppose you are a healthy young single man with a passion for downhill skiing. You haven't needed any medical care this year, but a month ago you damaged your knee during a winter vacation. The orthopedic surgeon you visit tells you that surgery can repair your knee.

Here's how the coverage would compare:

Indemnity. The orthopedic surgeon charges $100 for the consultation, and since this is your first medical bill of the year, you use it to satisfy your $100 deductible. You learn that the procedure to repair your knee plus follow-up care will cost well over $3,000. Your policy has a stop-loss of $3,000, which means that you will be responsible for paying your 20 percent share of the medical bills up to that amount. After that, the plan pays for 100 percent of your expenses, as long as they fall within UCR guidelines. According to this formula, the most you will have to pay toward physician and hospital expenses is 20 percent of $3,000, or $600. Add to that your $100 outlay to satisfy the deductible. Total out-of-pocket expense = $700.

PPO (using preferred providers). There is no deductible if you use preferred providers. By choosing a surgeon and hospital from the preferred list, you pay only 10 percent of your costs up to the $3,000 stop-loss ceiling. Total out-of-pocket expense = $300.

PPO (going outside the preferred list). If you want to use a surgeon or a hospital whose name does not appear on the preferred list, you can do so for a price. You would have to pay the $100 deductible, and your co-insurance rate would be less advantageous—30 percent rather than 10 percent. Let's say you choose both a surgeon and a hospital that are not on the preferred list. You would pay $100 plus 30 percent of the first $3,000 in medical expenses. Total out-of-pocket expense = $1,000.

HMO. Under the HMO's rules, you must use its physicians and hospitals. Your only expenses would be $3 co-payments for office visits: these would probably include a consultation with the surgeon plus three follow-up visits. Total out-of-pocket expense = $12.

The more important it is to you to choose your own obstetrician or surgeon, the more you will pay for that freedom of choice. The HMO offers you the best deal financially—but it also places the most restrictions on your choices.

In the knee surgery example, a decision to choose the indemnity plan would cost you $700. A decision to choose the PPO, using preferred providers, would cost you $300—and if you went outside the preferred list, $1,000—whereas care for the same problem in an HMO would cost you $12.

If freedom of choice is a paramount consideration, ask yourself *before* you sign up with a PPO whether you will be content with its preferred provider list. If you know which physicians and hospitals you would want to use, check to make sure they are on the preferred list. Otherwise, as you can see from this example, you might actually save money by choosing a traditional indemnity plan.

How much coverage would be available to you if you suffered a true catastrophe? Suppose you were in a devastating automobile accident that resulted in a lengthy hospitalization (including a week or two of intensive care); or you gave birth to a twenty-eight-week premature baby who had to stay in a neonatal intensive care unit for several months; or you developed a case of metastatic cancer that required extensive hospital stays as well as expensive outpatient chemotherapy or radiation treatment? Expenses for these kinds of problems can exceed $100,000.

When you compare plans for the protection they offer in this area, you need not concern yourself with small savings, such as a $100 difference in deductibles. Instead, you want to make sure that you would not run out of coverage when you needed it most. Check each plan to see if its stop-loss caps your expense at a level you can afford. Will you pay 20 percent of the first $5,000 of medical bills or 20 percent of the entire $100,000? Following are the critical areas to evaluate:

Indemnity plans. (1) Make sure the plan has a stop-loss (see chapter 1 for a discussion of this feature); (2) make sure it has a lifetime maximum of at least $250,000 and read the fine print to determine if the figure is inclusive. Some plans limit your coverage per diagnosis or per spell of illness; others put a limit on reimbursement by fixing it at a certain level per day for intensive care or neonatal intensive care; and (3) if the plan states that it limits coverage to "365 days of hospital care," read on! Such plans often require you to be *out* of the hospital for a defined interval, usually ninety days, before you can be covered for the next hospitalization. If you had a severe chronic problem, like metastatic cancer, you might run out of insurance if you signed up for a policy with this feature.

PPOs. A PPO is always paired with an indemnity option, and the PPO will have the same provisions as that plan. Thus, if the indemnity plan has a $3,000 stop-loss, so will the PPO. Because you have much lower co-insurance payments if you use providers and facilities from the preferred list, you will have better protection against catastrophic costs. Nevertheless, you must check the provisions of the companion indemnity plan to protect yourself from any surprises.

HMOs. All federally qualified HMOs provide unlimited hospital care, no lifetime maximum, and no caps in other areas, with two exceptions: they rarely cover extended hospitalization for psychiatric problems (more than 30 days) or for long-term rehabilitation after a stroke or spinal cord injury (more than 60 days).

Comparing Costs When You Have Special Needs

If you need coverage for mental health care, durable medical equipment, special medication, home care, or an unusual and expensive problem, you may find substantial financial differences between types of health insurance. Look carefully at each plan to see how well it would cover your own needs. In particular, check for exclusions for preexisting conditions.

Mental health. If you are currently in therapy and have reasonable coverage from an indemnity plan, ask some specific questions before you join an HMO. Most HMOs cover only acute problems that are amenable to short-term intervention. For example, an HMO would cover treatment for depression brought on by a divorce or death in the family but not treatment for a chronic personality disorder. If you have already been in therapy for some time, your subsequent care will probably not be covered because your problem would not fall under the definition "amenable to short-term intervention." Even if the plan agrees to provide therapy, you would have to see a therapist it authorized. To do so would almost always involve a potentially disruptive change in therapists.

If you have not entered treatment and are considering doing so, an HMO would cover you for a certain number of visits—a maximum of twenty per year is the usual number—and would probably charge you a co-payment for each visit, in the $10 to $20 range. Short-term treatment is effective for a wide range of problems and may be suitable for yours; if so, you will save a good deal of money by joining an HMO. Be aware that mental health practitioners hold widely divergent views; some therapists favor short-term treatment; others stress the importance of much longer interventions.

If your problem requires extensive treatment, and if you are otherwise healthy, indemnity insurance might be a good solution. Twenty-two percent of indemnity plans cover mental health care in the same way they cover other medical problems.[1] Most put mental health problems in a special category. Some will reimburse you for half the cost of your visit—with a ceiling on the total fee; others will reimburse you up to a maximum of $20 to $30 a visit. Since psychologists often charge $70 to $90 a visit and psychiatrists charge $90 to $120, you might have to pay costs of $40 or much more for each visit out of your own pocket.

Special medication. Unlike indemnity plans, most HMOs and a few PPOS have an approved list of drugs, known as a formulary. If you are considering an HMO and must take special or expensive medications, or if you prefer particular brand-name drugs, check with the HMO to see if the exact medications you want to use are on its approved list. (If the

HMO has its own pharmacies, you can call and speak to one of the plan's pharmacists. Otherwise, you can ask the plan's marketing representative for the name of an HMO staff member who can answer your questions.)

Most HMOs charge a small co-payment for each prescription, but they may not prescribe the same brand you use or they may substitute a generic drug. You will save money if the drugs they use are the ones you want. Otherwise, you must add to your out-of-pocket expense the cost of prescriptions the HMO does not fill.

Durable medical equipment. Wheelchairs, hospital beds, elaborate knee braces, and other types of equipment come under this category. In general, HMOs offer less coverage for these items than traditional insurance plans; 24 percent exclude them completely.[2] Traditional insurance usually covers durable medical equipment in the same way it does other expenses, subject to deductible, co-insurance, and UCR. If this category is important to you, find out exactly how the plans you are considering cover the equipment you need.

Home care. If you are homebound and have a chronic problem that requires skilled care from a health care professional (a licensed nurse, physical therapist, or occupational therapist, for example), an HMO will probably give you more generous coverage than other types of insurance would. Indemnity plans, for example, may contain provisions for home care coverage, but their benefits tend to be limited. Because HMOs are health care organizations as well as insurance plans, they can make arrangements to provide medical servicces in your home.

Emergency care. Indemnity policies, HMOs, and PPOs all cover the treatment of true emergencies (choking, severe bleeding, acute chest pain, severe burns, unconsciousness, convulsions, poisoning, and injuries that may cause permanent damage unless they are treated immediately), and you will be reimbursed no matter what hospital you go to. Your main concern would be to get to the nearest one as fast as possible.

Compare fees for emergency care. Two-thirds of HMOs

charge a co-payment for hospital emergency room visits, commonly $25. Many PPOs and some indemnity plans impose a separate emergency room deductible in the $25 to $100 range.

If you are considering an HMO, find out what happens if you make an honest mistake. For patients, the line between urgent care and emergency care may not be entirely obvious. Will you be reimbursed if, for example, you rush to the hospital with what you believe to be a heart attack, only to learn that you are suffering from severe indigestion? (See chapter 7 for tips on how to make sure you are reimbursed in this situation.)

Find out whether the plan will penalize you if someone else makes your medical decisions for you. For example, if you faint and someone takes you to a hospital emergency room, will your care be covered? Must you receive a specific diagnosis from the doctor at the emergency room in order to be covered?

Coverage while traveling. Indemnity plans, for the most part, offer unrestricted coverage while you are traveling. PPOS and HMOs are more restrictive, and if you spend a good deal of time away from the service area they cover, you may run into difficulties. Some HMOs belong to a network that allows members to seek care for urgent problems at any reciprocal HMO. If you travel frequently, this feature may be helpful.

All HMOs will cover your expenses if you need urgent care when you are out of town, but they may not reimburse you for care that could have waited. If, for example, your baby developed a bad earache while you were traveling, you could expect your bills from an out-of-town doctor and pharmacy to be reimbursed. But if instead you had her evaluated for a hearing problem, you would probably not be reimbursed. The plan would see this as care that could have waited. If you suffered a heart attack while traveling, the HMO would cover your expenses for treatment. If, after you recovered, the out-of-town physician recommended bypass surgery, the HMO would expect you to return to its service area for evaluation by one of its own physicians, provided you were well enough to travel.

Serious and expensive problems. If you are currently being treated for a serious medical problem, first make sure that any policy you are considering will cover it. Remember that some insurance plans have exclusions and waiting periods for preexisting conditions (PECs). People who sign up for health insurance through a large employer seldom encounter PECs, but those who work for small employers (fewer than 25 employees) usually do, and those who buy individual policies always do.

Once you've determined whether your problem is covered, you will want to confirm that the particular course of treatment you are undergoing will be covered. If you know that you will want to see a certain specialist or travel to a famous cancer center, examine each policy carefully and find out whether there are limitations on what doctors it will reimburse or what forms of treatment it will cover. A PPO or HMO may not authorize treatment from the physician or medical center you want to use. Indemnity plans may require you to seek prior authorization for certain kinds of treatment, and their UCR guidelines may fall far short of the fees you are paying. Some large employers contract with one or more nationally known medical centers to perform certain difficult and expensive procedures (typically, these are transplants) and require employees to use these centers if they want coverage under the company indemnity plan.

The Hazards of Mixing Fee-for-Service Expectations with HMO Care

Some people join an HMO without really understanding how a prepaid system works, thinking that the money they save on preventive services, routine check-ups, drugs, or lower premiums will fund fee-for-service care when they want it.

Suppose that Hal, a federal employee with two teenagers, determines that his family can save $30 a month on premiums and a sizable chunk on preventive care by joining an HMO. Neither Hal nor the two children has a personal physician. His wife, Betsy, intends to continue with her fee-for-service gynecologist, but she reasons that she can pay for those visits, with money to spare, out of the amount the family will save by using the other services of the HMO.

This approach works as long as Betsy doesn't develop any serious gynecological problem. But consider what would happen if she had a sudden onset of bleeding that required a D & C (dilation and curettage). She must then either switch to an HMO gynecologist or, if she continues to use her own gynecologist, pay all the expenses of the procedure out of her own pocket. It is unlikely that the HMO would reimburse her either for her physician's fees or for hospital bills when it did not arrange for, or authorize, the procedure.

Or suppose Betsy develops symptoms of endometriosis, for which her fee-for-service gynecologist recommends laparoscopy, a surgical procedure. Realizing how expensive this procedure will be, Betsy switches to an HMO gynecologist, who suggests she first try a nonsurgical treatment. Which doctor is right?

Is the fee-for-service doctor recommending laparoscopy because it is the correct next step or because she will make money by performing the procedure? Is the HMO gynecologist suggesting a nonsurgical approach purely in Betsy's interest, or is he trying to save money for the plan? As with many medical decisions, there may be more than one way to treat a problem. In this case, both physicians are offering reasonable courses of treatment, but Betsy will probably end up confused and upset. She may well have to choose between paying herself for care from her gynecologist or following the advice of the HMO physician if she wants insurance coverage.

You can avoid this sort of misunderstanding by asking questions before you choose a plan. For example, suppose that

Harry, who has had diabetes for many years, has received all his care from Dr. Berg, an endocrinologist. This year his company offers him the opportunity to join an HMO. When Harry talks to the HMO marketing representative, he learns that Dr. Berg is one of their consultants. He also finds out that his care will be fully covered; the HMO does not exclude preexisting conditions. So far, so good.

But when he asks about whether his regular visits to Dr. Berg will be covered, he learns that the plan uses her services only for difficult and complicated cases. Because his diabetes is well controlled, he is told that it can easily be managed by one of the plan's staff internists. Harry must now make up his mind about the HMO with clear knowledge that his care for diabetes will be handled differently.

Making Decisions about Dual Coverage

Dual coverage is the term used to describe a situation in which a person is covered under more than one policy. This most commonly occurs when a husband and wife are both employed and are both offered the opportunity to add dependents to the coverage provided by their respective employers.

Dual coverage for married couples without children. If you are a couple with no children and no plans to start a family, are fully covered by your own employers at no cost, and are able to add a spouse to your own plan at no extra charge, by all means sign each other up.

But if you must pay for dual coverage, carefully research how much additional coverage you will get for your money. Sometimes, dual coverage can offer significant financial protection. Let's assume that you are insured by your employer and that your spouse has added you to his or her plan. Your own indemnity plan has a $150 deductible, 80/20 coinsurance, and a stop-loss of $3,000. Now suppose you have a serious medical problem, with bills of $5,000.

Your insurance is termed the *primary* plan (you are the subscriber), and it pays $4,250, leaving you with an unreimbursed expense of $750 ($150 deductible, plus 20 percent of $3,000). You then submit the bills to your spouse's plan, which is called the *secondary* plan. It subtracts your deductible and pays for the 20 percent co-insurance, or $600. All you pay is $150.

Until recently, this was the way a typical dual coverage claim would be handled. Most insurance companies would not pay the deductible if their plan was secondary, but some would. All of them would reimburse you in full for your share of the co-insurance.

Now, as employers are looking for more ways to control health care costs, they are becoming more creative about cost-shifting. A number of plans include "carve-out" provisions, which allow them, when they are the secondary plan, to exclude any expense they would not have covered if they were the primary plan. If your spouse's employer has purchased a plan that does this, there is no advantage to dual coverage unless his or her plan has better coverage than yours.

In the above example, if your plan has no stop-loss, your liability would be 20 percent of $5,000, or $1,000. If your spouse's plan has a $3,000 stop-loss, even though it has a "carve-out" provision, it would reimburse you the $400 you paid for your co-insurance between the $3,000 ceiling and the $5,000 bill.

Thus, to decide whether it is worth signing up for dual coverage, you need to ask several questions:

- How much more will it cost?
- Does my spouse's plan have a "carve-out" provision, or will it reimburse me in full for my co-insurance payments?
- Does my primary coverage leave enough gaps (and/or do I use or expect to use so much medical care) that it is worth the extra premium dollars for dual coverage?

If there is a carve-out provision, the extra cost for dual coverage would not be worthwhile unless that cost is nominal or unless your own policy leaves you unprotected for large expenses; for example, if it does not contain a stop-loss provision.

Dual coverage for married couples with children. If both spouses are offered insurance by their employers, they need to decide which plan will cover other family members. One possibility is to enroll some or all of the family members in both plans. This dual coverage may offer you the opportunity to obtain much better financial protection at little extra cost.

First, find out which plan would be designated as the children's primary plan, and which would be secondary. In most states, insurance policies use the "birthday rule" and identify the plan of the parent whose birthday comes first in the calendar year as the primary plan. Some states use the "gender rule" and consider the father's plan to be primary. Check with your employer to find out what rule applies in your situation, as well as whether the plan that would be secondary has a "carve-out" provision.

Armed with the above information, you can calculate whether it is advantageous to buy secondary coverage for the children. You'll need, as usual, to determine how much coverage would be available under various scenarios. As a rule of thumb, it will be worth adding the children to the second plan if the cost is minimal, unless there is a "carve-out" provision.

Dual coverage offers important protection if you have a child with a serious medical condition. It will help pay for large medical expenses and will also improve your ability to continue comprehensive coverage if one spouse loses a job, if one of your employers reduces health insurance benefits, or if you divorce.

Coverage for children of divorced parents. If a divorce decree specifies that one parent is responsible for providing health insurance for the children, then that parent's plan will always be primary. In states with the gender rule, the father's plan is primary.

In states with the birthday rule, an unmarried parent who has custody is considered to be the primary policyholder. If the custodial parent remarries, the stepparent's plan is secondary, and the noncustodial parent's plan is tertiary. If parents have joint custody, the birthday rule applies.

Dual coverage for HMO members. Sometimes both husband and wife may have the opportunity to sign up their spouse and/or family members with the same HMO, as when both spouses are employed by a state government that offers an HMO plan, or, say, if both spouses are teachers within the same school system. Most HMOs will waive all co-payments for members who inform the HMO that they are "double-covered."

However, one spouse might want to choose the HMO family plan and the other sign up for an indemnity family plan. That way, if anyone in the family preferred a specialist or hospital not designated by the HMO, such care would be covered by the indemnity policy. As a rule of thumb, HMO coverage is so extensive that dual coverage is worthwhile only if the cost for the second family plan is negligible, or if the option to go outside the plan for care is particularly important.

Special Considerations If You Are Self-Employed

If you are self-employed, you can use the methods we have suggested to compare the coverage offered by the plans you are considering. The big difference you will encounter as an individual buyer is, of course, hefty charges for premiums. One strategy would be to select a high-deductible indemnity plan. This would protect you against catastrophic expenses while keeping premium costs as low as possible. (See chapter 1.)

If, however, you want more from your insurance than catastrophic coverage, you have two choices: you can buy a more expensive high-option indemnity policy that will give you better coverage for ordinary medical expenses, or you can try to find an HMO that offers membership to individuals and families who are not purchasing insurance through an employer. Joining an HMO would be especially worthy of consideration if you have young children, if you are planning to start a family, or if you use a lot of medical services. The coverage HMOs offer for prevention, routine care, and pregnancy is generally useful for young families, and HMO premiums will likely be the same or less than those for high-option indemnity plans.

However, finding an HMO that will enroll you may not be easy. Since statistics show that individuals who enroll in HMO plans tend to use much more medical care than those who sign up through employers, most HMOs have chosen not to offer their plans to individuals.

If you have the opportunity to choose among HMO plans, look for a plan that will give you a break on its rates. If, for example, you are young, an "age-rated" HMO—that is, one that keys the cost of the premium to the age of the subscriber—will be cheaper than a "community-rated" plan, which assigns everyone the same premium. Younger people are generally healthier and will therefore be assigned lower premiums. Some plans offer preferential rates to people who have good health habits.

If you join an HMO through your employer and then leave your employment, you can continue your HMO membership under COBRA provisions. (See chapter 1.)

Comparing Plans for Medical Quality and Service

Answers to the following questions will help you make comparisons among the different types of health plans you are considering.

Can I get an appointment when I want one and at a time that is convenient? As a general rule, doctors who practice in a fee-for-service setting will have better appointment availability for routine and non-urgent visits than doctors in a group practice HMO. Indemnity insurance plans, PPOs, and IPAs all work with fee-for-service physicians.

Will I be able to establish an ongoing relationship with a personal physician? If you see a fee-for-service doctor in solo practice, you can count on continuity of care (unless your doctor is on vacation or otherwise unavailable). Physicians in group practice may or may not emphasize continuity; the larger the group, whether it is prepaid or fee-for-service, the greater the chance that you will see a different doctor for at least some of your visits.

How far will I have to travel to reach the doctor's office? Is it easily reached by public transportation? If you will be driving, is there plenty of parking available?

Can I schedule doctors' visits before or after my working hours? As a rule, fee-for-service doctors tend to work regular business hours, although there is a trend toward providing Saturday hours. Many group practice HMOs offer evening appointments with primary care doctors, and some offer Saturday appointments as well.

What do I do when my doctor is unavailable? Most fee-for-service physicians make arrangements to share coverage with their colleagues or instruct the answering service to refer all patients who call after hours to the emergency room of the local hospital. With most indemnity plans, you are free to use any hospital emergency room you choose.

PPOs may give you a choice of using an urgent care clinic or a hospital emergency room. Be sure that the facilities on their preferred list are acceptable and convenient. You can, of course, go outside the preferred list, but it's likely to be an expensive decision.

Because they are responsible for their members' care at all times, HMOs generally have highly organized systems for dealing with urgent medical problems and provide twenty-four-hour telephone access to a physician, but members must *always* remember to call the plan *before* they seek care unless they experience a life-threatening emergency.

Can I easily get necessary X rays, lab work, and medications? If you are considering an indemnity plan, a PPO, or an IPA, you would save considerable time and energy if any of the physicians have lab, X-ray, and pharmacy services close at hand. Large fee-for-service group practices and HMO-affiliated group practices often provide these services in their centers. (With a PPO you must make sure that you receive these services in an approved facility.)

Special Considerations for HMOs

The more restrictions an insurance plan puts on your choice of providers and facilities, the more important it is for you to find out beforehand whether you will have access to good doctors and hospitals and whether you will receive prompt attention and convenient service.

If you buy indemnity insurance, you can easily change doctors if you are dissatisfied with the care you're getting. If you join a PPO, you can use a doctor whose name does not appear on the preferred list and settle for a lower rate of reimbursement.

But if you choose an HMO, it is especially important to satisfy yourself beforehand that the plan offers a high level of medical quality and service. Once you become a member, you must use its providers and services for a full year, and you'll receive no insurance coverage whatsoever if you seek care the plan has not approved.

Evaluating the Medical Quality of an HMO

The following questions will help you find and identify an HMO with a commitment to medical quality. Read them carefully and determine which are particularly pertinent to your needs and expectations. Then, ask the HMO's marketing representative to answer them in detail or arrange for you to speak with someone else in the organization who can.

Is the plan certified by an outside agency? Consider joining only those health maintenance organizations that are federally qualified or state certified. A plan that seeks formal approval from the federal government must satisfy the Office of Prepaid Health Care (OPHC) that it has a sound financial base, a well-organized medical delivery system, a formal quality assurance program, proper management, and legal protection against financial liability for its members should the plan fail. Inspection begins with a review of written materials submitted by the plan. If these are satisfactory, federal inspectors (including specialists in marketing, finance, management, and medical delivery systems) make a site visit to determine whether the written materials correspond with the reality. A plan that does not pass muster is given advice on what it must do to improve its operation.

Once an HMO is approved, or "federally qualified," it must continue to provide periodic reports, primarily on its marketing practices and financial status. The Office of Compliance (under the jurisdiction of OPHC) examines these reports and investigates those HMOs that do not appear to be living up to their obligations. Federal qualification may be revoked if serious deficiences are found; plans with less serious problems must remedy them within a specified period of time.

Standards vary among the states that certify HMOs. Usually, regulation on the business side falls to the state insurance commissioner, while the state department of health oversees the medical aspects. To find out whether your particular state has a certification program, call your state insurance commissioner. (The National Association of Insurance Commissioners has drawn up a model law that individual states can use as a basis for HMO regulation. See Appendix for a list of states that have adopted it.)

The advantage to the consumer of joining a federally qualified plan is that you know the plan offers extensive coverage and that it has a ceiling on out-of-pocket costs, a formal quality assurance program, a formal grievance mechanism, and protection for members should the HMO become insolvent. Although some well-established plans that are not federally qualified have excellent reputations, if you are considering joining such a plan you will need to assure yourself that all these elements are present. Pay particular attention to the thoroughness of the plan's quality assurance program, including the process it uses for credentialing and monitoring physicians, discussed in chapter 2.

Are the doctors well credentialed? Although credentials by themselves do not guarantee quality, they do provide reassurance that the physician staff is well trained. Any good plan will be happy to answer questions about its physicians' credentials. In a high-quality HMO, more than 90 percent of physicians will be board-certified or board-eligible. The plan may even require those who are board-eligible to pass their boards within two or three years of hiring in order to continue practicing in the HMO.

If you are unable to find an HMO that meets this standard, you might place a call to the county medical society in your area. Ask what percentage of physicians in your community are board-certified or board-eligible and look for an HMO that at least meets, if not exceeds, your community standard. (See chapter 3 for a discussion of medical credentials.)

Find out from the HMO's marketing representative if plan physicians are involved with medical education or research. Do some of them hold faculty positions at a medical school? Is the HMO a site for the teaching or training of medical students or residents? Do its physicians engage in research or produce articles for medical journals? Does it organize in-house educational programs for its medical staff? Is it sponsored by or affiliated with a medical school or a highly respected group practice? "Yes" answers to several of these questions would be positive signs of medical quality.

Many group practice HMOs can supply you with directories that list each physician's credentials. If you are considering signing up with an IPA model HMO because your own primary care physician is affiliated, you can ask your doctor's opinion about the quality of specialists and hospitals associated with the plan. If, however, you are going to be choosing a new doctor, you can save yourself work by narrowing the list of doctors affiliated with the plan to the primary care physicians that you would be most likely to use (depending on their location and type of practice). You can then ask the HMO about the credentials of those doctors on your short list. (In chapter 2, you will find a discussion of how good HMOs evaluate physicians.)

All specialists affiliated with the plan should be board-certified and should be members of their respective specialty societies. It is desirable for them to be affiliated with teaching hospitals and even better for them to be involved in medical teaching or supervision. An HMO that contracts with specialists in the community may list physicians you recognize and respect; their association with the plan would be further assurance of the plan's medical quality.

Does the plan contract with good hospitals? Before you join, find out what hospitals the plan uses. Make sure any hospital the plan would send you to is fully accredited by the JCAHO. If the plan uses hospitals that fail to meet this minimum requirement, don't join.

Find out whether the plan uses teaching hospitals (those hospitals that serve as training sites for interns and residents). A hospital that serves as a site for medical education must meet rigorous national standards.

Perhaps your best guarantee of the quality of the HMO's hospitals is the quality of its physician staff. It is an axiom of the medical profession that good doctors insist on working in good hospitals; therefore, if you have determined that a particular plan has a reputation for good medical care and that it hires well-trained doctors, you can conclude that the hospitals it uses are likely to be well run.

If an HMO uses more than one hospital, will I be able to choose the one I prefer? A plan may list two hospitals, one a community hospital and the other a major medical center, but it may not give you the choice. Its physicians may use the medical center for neurosurgery, cardiac surgery, and other complex procedures and send HMO members to the community hospital for childbirth and most elective surgery.

Your ability to choose your hospital may depend on the doctor you select. A plan that serves a large geographical area may list a number of hospitals, but a physician affiliated with the plan may practice at only one or two of them. Check the list of physicians before you join and find out whether those you want to use admit their patients to the hospital you would prefer.

If I have an unusual and very serious problem, will I be referred to a major out-of-town medical center? One common concern of people considering an HMO is whether or not they would be referred to "the best hospital" if they had a very serious condition. If, for instance, you would want to go to The Cleveland Clinic, and only there, for bypass surgery, you should not join an HMO. This procedure can be performed proficiently at hundreds of hospitals around the country—and the same holds true of many other procedures.

While no HMO will promise you the medical center of your choice, many good HMOs do pay to send patients out of town for problems that cannot be adequately treated at local facilities. Some highly specialized procedures—liver transplants, for example—are performed at only a handful of institutions. Ask whether the HMO you are considering has sent patients with unusual problems to well-known medical centers. If you learn that this happens on occasion, you may find the knowledge reassuring.

Does the plan have an active quality assurance program? HMOs with high medical standards put a good deal of effort into monitoring and improving the care that members receive. (See chapter 2 for further information on this topic.)

Does the plan make sure I can get medical care in a timely fashion? You should be able to get a routine appointment within two weeks and an urgent appointment within twenty-four hours. The plan should reserve appointment slots for people who need immediate medical attention. You should also be able to call your physician directly if you have an urgent medical problem.

How difficult is it to get appointments with a specialist? If your primary care physician believes that it's important for you to see a specialist immediately, you should be able to get an appointment within forty-eight hours. Find out if you will have a choice of specialists.

Are mid-level practitioners properly used and supervised? If you receive care from a mid-level practitioner (physician assistant, nurse practitioner), he or she should be able to consult a physician on the spot should questions arise during a visit. Patients who prefer to see a physician should not be pressured to use a mid-level practitioner. (For further information on mid-levels, see chapter 3.)

How does the plan deal with abnormal lab results? Relying on the patient to call in for lab results is not sufficient; good doctors in any type of practice make earnest efforts to reach patients who have had abnormal results. This is a tricky issue, since providers must maintain confidentiality and can give results only to patients. Nevertheless, the obstacles posed by keeping results confidential should not be presented as an excuse for failing to have an active outreach program.

Does the plan identify problems and organize programs to address them? Plans with a commitment to medical quality and service analyze the problems of their patient population and create programs that address the areas of greatest need. For example, HMOs have developed programs to prevent premature births, educate diabetics, provide coordinated care to teenagers, and reduce adverse drug interactions.

Quality of Service

To obtain information about the quality of service a plan offers, ask the following questions of the HMO's marketing representative:

Are medical facilities conveniently located? Is there adequate parking? Does the plan offer "one-stop" medical care? Most group practice HMOs have multipurpose health care centers. Some or all of the group practices in a group network plan will also operate well-equipped centers.

Will I be seen promptly once I arrive for an appointment? Many HMOs have measured the average length of time patients must wait before they are seen, and you should ask for this information. In general, obstetrical and surgical patients may have longer waits because their doctors are called away to the hospital more often than other physicians. A reasonable office wait would be fifteen minutes, and you should not expect to have to spend longer than thirty minutes after the time of your appointment unless a serious emergency has occurred.

How long will I have to wait for routine screening tests and routine physicals? Find out how long you might have to wait for the screening tests you need. The plan may have developed guidelines that identify how often screening tests should be done based on your age, sex, and specific risk factors, and it may do active outreach for certain types of preventive screening. You should be able to schedule promptly those tests the plan recommends.

If you know that you will want a routine physical, find out how long you will have to wait to schedule one. Many plans, especially during a busy enrollment period, may have waits as long as six to eight weeks for people with no special health problems or concerns.

How will I get after-hours care? Urgent care (for an acute problem that is not an emergency but requires immediate attention) may be handled differently depending on the arrangements made by a particular plan. You may be sent to a health care center that is open late, a free-standing urgent care center, or a designated hospital emergency room.

How do I go about selecting and changing doctors? Group practice plans, and those IPAs that use the "case-manager" approach, will ask you to choose a primary care physician from their roster of physicians. The list may be fairly limited or very extensive, depending on the size and type of plan you are considering. To make sure patients have access to their physicians, many HMOs keep track of a physician's complement of patients, or "panel," and list it as closed if waits for appointments would otherwise be too long. If you are considering joining a group practice model HMO because of the reputation of a particular physician, make sure before you join that the physician is taking new patients. Physicians who contract with IPA model HMOs will continue seeing their fee-for-service patients who switch to HMO coverage, but they may not be accepting new HMO patients. All HMOs will allow you to change physicians during your membership, but the way you go about it will vary from plan to plan.

What does the plan do for prospective members? Most group practice plans encourage prospective members to visit a health care center. An attractive, orderly, and friendly atmosphere tells you the plan has put time, effort, and concern into its operations. Find out if an open house is scheduled; this would offer a good opportunity to have your questions answered. If you are choosing between two different group practice plans, visit one of each plan's health care centers.

Does the plan offer health education services? Group practice HMOs with a strong service orientation will offer a number of free or low-cost classes for weight control, stopping smoking, parenting, childbirth education, and so on, as well as support groups for people with specific medical problems. In addition, some HMOs now offer a personal health risk assessment to help members identify ways to improve their health and prevent disease.

Is the plan responsive to customers? Customer responsiveness should be built into all of the plan's systems and should be reflected in the behavior of both its clinical and its business staff. The marketing representatives are the first employees of the plan that you will meet; they should be knowledgeable about what they are selling and should be willing to find answers to questions they cannot answer themselves.

What kind of orientation program is available for new members?

The plan should provide help in choosing a physician and in understanding how to use the system. Ask if the plan has a member handbook, and look through it to see if the system is clearly explained.

How concerned is the plan with patient complaints? The plan you join should have a clearly defined system for recording and resolving members' complaints. A consumer-responsive plan will work hard to keep members satisfied, and it will attempt to resolve problems before members demand a formal hearing. Some plans use consumer committees to review all serious complaints on a formal basis. All federally qualified HMOs must, by law, have a formal grievance process.

It is difficult to quantify how many complaints signal that an HMO is failing to please its customers. Some plans encourage a formal recording and review of all complaints; others focus on resolving as many as possible on the spot.

Group practice plans should have a designated staff member (often called a "member service representative" or "patient representative") at each health care center to deal with service problems as they arise. IPAs should assign a member of their central administrative staff to handle complaints and solve problems.

The formal grievance process exists for those members who have attempted to solve disagreements informally, without success. The process usually includes a series of appeals—to the medical director of the plan, then to the president, and possibly to a special grievance committee of the board of directors. In some HMOs, members of the plan sit on the board grievance committee. This kind of involvement would be an especially reassuring sign that a plan is serious about giving those who belong a fair hearing.

Most of the cases that come before a grievance committee involve disputes over what the contract covers. For example, the HMO may have denied coverage for a procedure because it deemed it purely cosmetic, or it may have refused to pay a bill for an out-of-area claim because the problem could have waited until the member returned to the HMO's service area.

The grievance system is not used for issues of possible professional liability, which in most states are dealt with no differently for HMO members than for anyone else. California, however, allows HMOs to require their members at the time they enroll in a plan to agree to binding arbitration of malpractice claims.

If you are employed, your benefits specialist may have information on how well the HMOs it offers have handled complaints made by employees of your company. If you are planning to join as an individual subscriber, try calling the office of the insurance commissioner for your state, and ask how many complaints have been received in the past year and whether they reflect a common theme. This kind of specific information may or may not be recorded, depending on the state in which you live.

Has the HMO done any consumer satisfaction studies? A good HMO cares about the attitudes of its members and looks for ways to improve service. Find out whether the plan has done a survey recently and request to see the tabulation of results. (The better the plan, the easier it will be to obtain this information.) You will need to look at the numbers realistically. No system yet devised has 100 percent satisfaction; good results would be in the 80 percent range.

Organizational Stability

You can ask the marketing representative for an annual report, call the Better Business Bureau, or find out how many years the plan has been in existence, but none of these measures will give you bottom-line information about how well managed the plan is.

What financial protection do I have if the plan fails? If you are thinking of joining a local HMO or one that is new on the national scene, ask what provisions the plan has made to protect you if it experiences a business failure. (See chapter 2 for a discussion of insolvency protection.)

What is the turnover rate for physicians and senior managers? A low rate of physician turnover, under 10 percent a year, is desirable. Find out how long the chief executive officer, medical director, marketing director, operations director, and finance director have been with the organization. Three or more years for at least two of them would show acceptable continuity.

Have there been steep premium increases? HMOs must contend with the same rising health care costs that are causing all insurance plans to increase their premiums rapidly. However, over a period of years, a well-managed HMO should be able to keep its average rate increase well below 15 percent, even though the increase in any one year may be 20 percent or more. Several years of such increases might indicate that the plan's management is not able to control costs effectively while maintaining quality.

In some cases, what appear to be steep increases in HMO rates are actually the result of an employer's decision, not an HMO's. Some employers peg the employees' cost of health insurance contributions to the least expensive plan they offer. Let's assume that one year an employer offers an indemnity policy that costs $220 a month and an HMO plan that costs $230. The employer may decide to pay $200 of the indemnity policy and have the employees contribute $20. The employer then pays the same $200 toward the $230 premium of its HMO plan, leaving the employees who wish to join with a $30 contribution.

But if, like most businesses, the company is looking for ways to save money on insurance, the next year the benefits department may find a less expensive indemnity plan that costs $210; this now becomes the least expensive plan. The company can decide to charge its employees the same $20 contribution it required the previous year, thereby lowering the company's contribution toward the cheapest plan to $190. If that year the HMO raises its rates from $230 to $250 (an increase of less than 9 percent) the employees who choose the HMO will be required to contribute the difference between $250 and the employer's contribution of $190, or $60.

This increase would appear to employees to be a 100 percent jump in HMO rates.

Does the plan participate in national organizations? We would be wary of a plan that does not belong to one of the three national HMO industry groups: Group Health Association of America (GHAA—not to be confused with individual HMOs named Group Health), the American Managed Care and Review Association (AMCRA), or The HMO Group. These industry-wide groups share information about national trends, offer workshops and training programs for member HMOs, and lobby for HMO interests. An HMO that did not belong to one of these groups would be demonstrating a remarkable lack of interest in its own field of endeavor.

Sources of Information

Where do you take the long list of questions we have given you? Obviously, you will learn all you can from questioning the HMO marketing representative, reading the literature the HMO distributes, and talking to your company benefits administrator—or your insurance agent. You can ask for a copy of the member handbook, which will answer some of the questions we have raised here, such as where health care centers are located, what hours the centers are open, what to do when you need care after hours, what defines an emergency, and how soon the plan must be notified of any emergency or out-of-area care you have received. After that, what do you do?

Fee-for-service physicians can, in some situations, be good resources. If you are considering joining an IPA because your physician is on its list, he or she may have had enough experience with the plan to offer some useful opinions. Ask whether other patients who are HMO members are pleased with the plan. If, however, you are considering joining a group practice plan, remember that you may be putting a physician on the spot by asking him or her to endorse the competition.

You can make sure a plan is federally qualified by writing or calling the Office of Prepaid Health Care (OPHC). The National Association of Employers with Health Care Alternatives (NAEHCA) publishes a directory of HMOs, as does InterStudy, an organization that analyzes health care issues. (See Appendix for addresses of these organizations.) Your state's insurance commissioner or health commissioner will have addresses of various plans within the state.

Any HMO you are considering should be willing to supply you with information beyond what is contained in its marketing brochures. Annual reports, previous issues of member newsletters, even a copy of the subscriber contract should be available to you upon request. In addition, the plan should identify someone who can answer your questions. If you suspect that the marketing representative is pushing you into joining without listening to your concerns, call the office of the marketing director and ask whether the people who sell the plan receive a significant part of their income in commissions or whether they work on salary.

Your company's benefits department may be a rich source of information. Some large national companies, among them General Motors, Xerox, and J. C. Penney, do their own in-depth evaluations of the HMOs they offer their employees, and their benefits staff may be able to provide answers to almost any question about an HMO they have reviewed. Smaller companies may arrange for a consultant to do such an evaluation of the HMOs they offer and can provide you with information about any plan you are considering. Unless the HMO is being offered for the first time, your company's benefits administrators will have had experience in dealing with the plan and may be able to tell you how employees who use the HMO rate the care and service.

Making Your Choice: Factoring in Your Attitudes and Preferences

If you read a policy thoroughly, perform the calculations we suggest, and ask enough questions, you can make a reasonable estimate of what you're buying with your premium dollars. But factors such as convenience and service are more difficult to quantify, and these less tangible aspects of medical care may make a big difference in how satisfied you will be with the plan you choose. When you are ready to make your final choice, here are some issues to consider beyond hard dollar comparisons.

Your present medical relationships. A good doctor-patient relationship is the foundation of good health care. If you have a trusted and well-qualified personal physician, we recommend that you choose an insurance plan that allows you to continue with him or her. Assuming that the cost of the premium is not an issue, this recommendation will be easy to follow if you are generally in good health, since your medical expenses will be minimal.

If, however, you should begin to need a good deal of medical care, financial pressures might lead you to give up that long-standing relationship in exchange for an HMO's more comprehensive coverage. Remember, though, that it is just when you are sick that your relationship with a doctor is especially comforting and helpful. If you need to save money, you might be able to join an IPA or a PPO with which your doctor is affiliated.

Your attitude toward paperwork. Some people loathe filling out forms, while others regard them as merely a minor nuisance or as a kind of sporting challenge. As we have pointed out, you must be disciplined about filling out forms if you are to take full advantage of your indemnity coverage. If you dislike paperwork, remember that it's even harder to do when you are worried or sick.

HMOs do not require you to fill out forms for authorized care. Some PPOs demand a very minimal level of paperwork because they have no deductible and have arranged for their preferred providers to bill you only for your percentage of co-insurance.

Your willingness to be assertive. Using any form of insurance to your maximum advantage will require some assertiveness. With an indemnity insurance policy, you must be willing to discuss fees with your physician and to find out whether your policy sets a ceiling on physicians' fees in the form of a fee schedule or UCR charges. You may have to do some negotiating either to convince your doctor to accept what the insurance company pays or to convince the insurance company that you are a special case.

People who have trouble discussing money will be reluctant to raise financial issues with the physician they are counting on to cure their ills. Even those who are prepared to discuss payment problems may encounter a doctor who is ill at ease or downright intimidating.

Assertiveness may save you money in a PPO as well. Be prepared to question doctors to make sure that the care they order—lab work, X rays, consultations with other physicians—comes from providers on the preferred list. Some physicians sign up with a number of plans but fail to develop office systems to track which patient is on which plan.

In an HMO, a different kind of assertiveness may be necessary in order to get routine appointments when you want them. If you are worried about your health but do not have symptoms that indicate you need immediate attention, you may need to talk to a screening nurse or a patient service representative to obtain a prompt appointment.

Peace of mind. Which insurance plan will do the best job of reducing your anxiety about paying for medical care? Suppose you have signed up for an indemnity plan with a sizable deductible. You know that until you have met your deductible, you must decide each time you have a medical problem or concern whether it is serious enough to warrant the cost of a visit to the doctor. If you don't like making these kinds of decisions, an HMO or a PPO with no deductible may be worth more than straight financial calculations show.

HMOs and PPOs can provide peace of mind at the other extreme, too. If you should develop an unexpectedly serious medical problem, you may face large out-of-pocket expenses. As we discussed on page 139, under Mutual Providential's indemnity policy, with a $100 deductible and a $3,000 stop-loss, you would be responsible for $600 in medical bills, plus the $100 deductible. If your doctor's fees for the treatment you received were higher than those recognized by the insurance plan as usual, customary, and reasonable, you would be responsible for paying the additional amounts yourself. (PPO members who use nondesignated providers are also responsible for paying 100 percent of any portion of a fee that is higher than that allowed by the insurance company.)

Making Trade-offs

The following chart summarizes the basic characteristics of different types of health insurance and helps you focus on the kinds of trade-offs you must make in the process of choosing a plan. Types of plans are listed from left to right in order of increasing breadth of coverage, increasing financial protection, increasing efforts to screen physicians and monitor quality, and *decreasing* freedom of choice.

The chart also shows you where your "choice point" occurs with each type of plan and how frequently you are able to exercise choice. The greater the financial penalty you must pay for freedom of choice, the more you will want to make sure that the plan you choose offers good doctors and hospitals.

At the far left is "unmanaged indemnity," or unrestricted indemnity insurance—the kind of plan that was dominant in 1980 but is rapidly disappearing. Next to it is "managed indemnity," which has the kinds of restrictions (second surgical opinions, prior authorization, and so on) discussed under "cost managing" in the Introduction. For people who want to retain the freedom to make all their own medical choices—of personal physicians, specialists, hospitals—and wish to do so with the fewest rules, indemnity insurance is the best choice.

For some people, the task of selecting physicians from the community at large seems chancy and burdensome. They would prefer a medical system that prescreens and monitors physicians and that takes responsibility for selecting specialists, hospitals, and other medical services. For them, the most tightly controlled plan, the group practice HMO, is ideal.

Those people who want most of the financial advantages of a group practice HMO, but prefer greater choice, may decide to sign up with an IPA model HMO or a PPO. Both types of plans will usually offer you a wide selection of primary care physicians. Many PPOs will allow you to refer yourself to specialists, but some are "gatekeeper" plans that require you to have prior approval from a primary care physician. A few IPAs still allow self-referral to specialists, but most now utilize gatekeepers.

Some people feel hampered by having to choose from a restricted list of providers, but they no longer have the option of selecting an indemnity plan. Other people don't mind a restricted choice for most problems, but they like the reassurance of knowing that they can seek care from outside providers on occasion without giving up all their coverage. For both of these groups, either a PPO or an HMO with a self-referral option would offer, for a price, an escape hatch into the free choice of an indemnity plan.

USUAL CHARACTERISTICS OF HEALTH INSURANCE PLANS

	Unmanaged Indemnity	Managed Indemnity	Preferred Provider Insurance (PPI)	PPI with Gatekeeper	HMO with Self-Referral Option*	IPA/Network HMO	IPA/Network HMO with Gatekeeper	Group Practice HMO
Choice point	Time of service	Time of service	Time of service	Time of service	Time of service	Annual	Annual	Annual
Can continue with present physicians	Yes	Yes	Maybe	Maybe	Yes	Maybe	Maybe	No
Can see specialist without primary care physician referral	Yes	Yes	Yes	No	Yes	Yes	No	No
Coverage for specialists seen without referral	Subject to deductible and co-insurance	Subject to deductible and co-insurance	90–100% if in network; otherwise, subject to deductible and co-insurance	Subject to deductible and co-insurance	Subject to deductible and co-insurance	100% if in network; otherwise, none	None	None
Pre-authorization required for elective surgery, hospitalization, etc.	No	Yes	Yes	Yes	Yes	Yes	Yes	Yes
Out-of-pocket costs (deductible, co-insurance, co-payments)	High	High	Low to moderate if in network; otherwise, high	Low to moderate if in network; otherwise, high	High	Low	Low	Low

Comprehensive coverage (prevention, screening, drugs)	Seldom	Seldom	Often	Often	Seldom	Yes	Yes	Yes
Selection process for physicians	No program	No program	+ to + +	+ to + +	No program	+ +	+ + +	+ + + +
Quality assurance program	No program	No program	+	+	No program	+ +	+ + +	+ + + +

Note: To characterize certain areas, we have used a 1+ to 4+ system, with 1+ representing the least (but more than "none") and 4+ the most. When there is quite a bit of variation, we have indicated a range (e.g., + to + +).
*When member does not use HMO providers.

6

Buying Coverage to Supplement Medicare

When Medicare was created in 1965, it represented a troubled compromise, patched together despite the incompatible goals of those who enacted the legislation. Its supporters, concerned about rapidly rising medical costs, wanted to create a plan that would protect older people on fixed incomes from a system that forced them to spend all their personal resources on medical care before being eligible for funds from public assistance. Opponents of the program argued for a voluntary health insurance program that would be supported by government funds.

There was considerable disagreement even among those who favored Medicare. Many of its advocates did not want older people to regard it as "charity" and insisted that its benefits be identical for everyone, regardless of income. Others feared that an attempt to provide comprehensive insurance to the entire elderly population would dilute the benefits, making it impossible to offer extensive coverage to those who were most in need.

The Medicare Act of 1965 emerged from heated congressional debate with age as its principal eligibility requirement. Everyone over sixty-five could sign up for Medicare, with no test to determine need. To satisfy those in Congress who were concerned about funding such a sweeping program, the plan was designed to provide only partial coverage. At that time, medical costs were not nearly as high as now, and Medicare usually covered a large share, if not most, of a beneficiary's bill. As medical costs have increased, the federal government's outlays for Medicare have soared—from $3.2 billion in 1967 to nearly $88 billion in 1988.

A 1989 article in *Consumer Reports* maintained that

> Medicare was held hostage to the charge of "socialized medicine"—the rallying cry of its political opponents, led by the American Medical Association, the American Hospital Association, and other arms of organized medicine. To overcome that charge, Medicare's proponents finally chose as their model for paying hospitals and doctors the system long used by Blue Cross and Blue Shield plans, insurance reimbursement systems designed by organized medicine itself. Under this "fee-for-service" model, hospitals and doctors set their own "reasonable and customary" fees, and the Blues paid them, rarely asking any questions.[1]

Using this approach, Congress designed Medicare to pay only up to a maximum fee, which varied by community and physician, leaving the patient to pay 100 percent of the "excess" physician fees above the Medicare maximum. The hope was that physicians would accept the Medicare rate as payment in full. Most have not.

Costs to Medicare beneficiaries have also skyrocketed. Along with the rising costs of physician fees, other expenses have risen far in excess of general inflation. In 1966, for example, the Medicare deductible for hospitalization was set at $40, which represented the average cost of a day in the hospital. By 1990, this deductible soared to $592. Medicare does not provide enough assistance to those who need its protection the most, requiring beneficiaries to pay a deductible for both hospital and physician care and co-insurance for all physician care and for extended hospitalization. Many older people who can ill afford supplementary insurance must somehow find money to buy it or face bankrupting themselves in order to qualify for public assistance for expensive medical care.

In 1988 Congress tried to plug some of the holes in Medicare by passing the Medicare Catastrophic Coverage Act. This short-lived piece of legislation extended coverage for hospitalization, but it did little to protect beneficiaries from large physicians' bills and the costs of medication, and nothing to protect them from exactly what its name implied: the "catastrophic costs" of long-term care in a nursing home. Yet another political compromise led to the decision to fund 100 percent of the new benefits by charging beneficiaries additional premiums and surtaxes on their incomes. This feature generated a storm of opposition, and most of the added coverage was repealed in 1989.

Now that the dust is settling, the basic flaws of the program remain. People must still buy supplementary policies if they can afford them; many others less fortunate end up with public assistance, even though protection from that eventuality was the original intent of the Medicare program.

The Basics of Medicare Coverage

Because Medicare is such an elaborate system of rules and exceptions, we cannot hope to explain every single aspect of the program here. What follows is a summary of those features that you need to understand before you can make a knowledgeable choice of a supplementary policy. We have emphasized those conditions for reimbursement and gaps in coverage that are especially important to keep in mind as you compare various "Medigap" plans, as these policies to supplement Medicare are commonly called. (See Appendix for further reading on Medicare.)

Medicare's Two-Part Structure

All Medicare is divided into two parts. *Part A*, which is paid for out of a hospital trust fund financed by a special payroll tax, covers most care in hospitals and, to some extent, care in skilled nursing facilities and in the home. Part A expenses are subject to a deductible and various co-payments. There is no premium charged to beneficiaries for Part A coverage.

Part B covers the cost of physician fees in and out of the hospital as well as the costs of diagnostic tests, ambulance services, and various types of outpatient services. Medicare pays 80 percent of allowable charges; beneficiaries are responsible for the remaining 20 percent, but they must pay any charges in excess of the fees allowed by Medicare. Medicare also covers mental health treatment provided by a psychiatrist, Ph.D. psychologist, or certified social worker at 50 percent of allowable charges. Although there has been no coverage for wellness care or preventive services in the past, as of July 1, 1990, Medicare covers an annual pap test.

For Part B coverage, beneficiaries pay $28.60 per month in 1990, which is deducted from their Social Security checks. This charge represents 25 percent of the cost of providing Part B coverage; the remaining 75 percent comes from general revenues that flow into a supplementary medical insurance trust fund. The beneficiaries' monthly charge is subject to adjustment each year.

Everyone who is eligible for Social Security receives Part A coverage at no cost. If you want Part B coverage, you must sign up for it and pay a separate monthly premium.

Part A Coverage: Hospitalization and Skilled Nursing Care

Hospitalization. Part A covers 100 percent of the cost of the first 60 days of hospitalization after the beneficiary pays a deductible ($592 in 1990). This deductible is indexed to overall increases in medical costs, and it will increase each year.

Part A coverage includes the cost of a semiprivate room, lab and X-ray services, nursing, meals, drugs from the hospital pharmacy, medical supplies, appliances, and operating and recovery room charges. Inpatient psychiatric care is covered up to a lifetime maximum of 190 days. A separate deductible is required for blood transfusions. Patients must pay for the cost of three pints or find a way to replace them—for instance, by having family members make donations to a local blood bank.

Once a hospitalization extends beyond sixty days, beneficiaries must begin to make co-payments. The specific amounts are based on a percentage of the deductible, and the actual figures will change each year. The following chart summarizes the way hospitalization is reimbursed under Part A.

HOSPITAL COVERAGE UNDER MEDICARE IN 1990

Length of Admission	Charge to Beneficiaries
Day 1	$592*
Days 2 through 60	None
Days 61 through 90	$148 per day
Days 91 through 150**	$296 per day
Days 151 and beyond	Full hospital charges

*No deductible if you are hospitalized within 60 days of a previous hospital discharge.

**Beneficiaries receive 60 "lifetime reserve days." These days can be applied only to a hospitalization that lasts longer than ninety days, and they can be used only once in a lifetime. For these days, the co-payment is set at 50 percent of the deductible. *For example, a beneficiary who has a hospitalization that lasts 130 days will pay $296 a day (in 1990) for days 91 through 130. Upon discharge, he or she will have used up 40 of the 60 lifetime reserve days. If the next year another extended hospital stay is necessary, Medicare coverage would be exhausted after day 110.*

Benefit period. Medicare starts the clock when you enter the hospital and keeps it running if you transfer to a skilled nursing facility or a rehabilitation facility. The period of time during which you receive care is called a "benefit period." In order to renew full Part A benefits, you must have a sixty-day interval following your discharge from the hospital, skilled nursing facility, or rehabilitation facility during which you do not receive care in any of these institutions. For example, a beneficiary who goes home after a hospitalization that lasts 45 days and is readmitted before 60 days have elapsed will have only 15 more days of full coverage. Starting with the sixteenth day, a $148 a day (in 1990) co-payment will be charged.

Skilled nursing care. Medicare Part A covers a specified amount of "skilled care." *It must be ordered by a physician and provided by a licensed nurse in a Skilled Nursing Facility (SNF).* Such a facility must be licensed by the state, must keep daily medical records, and must have twenty-four-hour nursing care available. Unless it meets these criteria, it is not considered a SNF. Patients who require rehabilitation *will not be reimbursed for care they receive in an Intermediate Care Facility (ICF).* (ICFs are institutions that for the most part provide rehabilitation services to patients who are generally more mobile than those in SNFs.)

In order to be eligible for SNF benefits, a beneficiary must spend at least three days in the hospital and must enter the SNF within thirty days of discharge. Patients in SNFs generally require intensive nursing care. For example, they may require intravenous medication or chemotherapy, or need to be fed through a feeding tube. SNF care must be related to the condition the beneficiary was treated for in the hospital.

Coverage is restricted to one hundred days in a benefit period. The first twenty days of SNF care are covered in full. Days twenty-one to one hundred are subject to a co-payment indexed to medical inflation ($74 a day in 1990). As with hospital coverage, sixty days must elapse after completion of your treatment before you are once again eligible for 100 days of SNF coverage.

Home health care. Medicare will pick up 100 percent of the tab for skilled nursing care, speech therapy, and physical therapy if you are homebound. There is no limitation on "intermittent" care (defined as care in the home that is rendered no more than four days a week). A physician must renew orders for intermittent care every sixty days. If a physician certifies that you require daily care, he or she has to renew the order every twenty-one days.

Services and medical equipment for home health care must be ordered and regularly reviewed by a physician and must be provided by a home health care agency that has been certified by Medicare. Medicare pays in full for home health care that is covered and pays 80 percent of what it deems allowable charges for durable medical equipment such as hospital beds and wheelchairs.

Part B Coverage: Physicians' Charges

To receive Part B coverage you must pay a monthly premium. This premium, as mentioned, is $28.60 in 1990. Your Part B coverage begins after you pay a $75 deductible.

Physicians' fees If you have enrolled for Part B coverage, Medicare will pay 80 percent of "Medicare allowable charges." Medicare bases the allowable charge on the lowest of: (1) what your doctor actually charged you; (2) your doctor's customary charge for the service; or (3) the prevailing charge for the service among physicians in your community. Medicare's calculations are complicated, and Medicare intermediaries utilize millions of bits of information in their computers to arrive at the allowable charge. The calculations may, in fact, produce allowable charges that vary from patient to patient for the same service in the same community. As you compare supplementary insurance policies, bear in mind that *any amount you are billed in excess of the "allowable charge" will not be covered by Medicare and will be your responsibility.* Bear in mind, too, that there is *no* stop-loss for physicians' bills.

Beginning in 1991, excess charges will be limited to 25 percent of Medicare allowable charges. In 1992, that number will decline to 20 percent, and after that, it will drop to 15 percent.

Medications. Medicare has extremely limited coverage for outpatient medications. It covers home intravenous drugs as part of the Medicare durable medical equipment (DME) benefit if the drugs are necessary for the effective use of the equipment, and it covers immunosuppressive drugs for a year after an organ transplant that was paid for by Medicare. Otherwise, there is no coverage for prescription drugs.

Long-term nursing-home care. *Medicare does not cover the costs of care in the kinds of custodial institutions or Health Related Facilities (HRFs) that people often refer to as "nursing homes."*

What Medicare Does Not Cover

Medicare alone does not provide enough protection for its beneficiaries. In fact, people over the age of sixty-five now pay a higher percentage of their medical expenses than they did before the program went into effect. Without additional insurance, the uncovered costs generated by one serious illness—deductibles, co-insurance, excess charges from physicians who do not accept Medicare's fee schedule, prescription drugs—can run to thousands of dollars.

If you are working, you can subscribe to group insurance coverage through your employer. You do not have to pay for Part B until you are no longer covered by your employer. If you are retired, your former employer may be paying for coverage to supplement Medicare. Nonetheless, you should compare the supplemental coverage and premium cost of the plan supplied by your employer with the other supplemental policies available to determine whether other supplemental policies offer more coverage for the same or less expense.

In 1990 the National Association of Insurance Commissioners set new minimum benefits standards for Medigap plans. Policies must cover the hospital co-payments for days 61–90 and for lifetime reserve days, the 20 percent of Medicare-approved charges for doctors, and at least 90 percent of Medicare-approved expenses for 365 days of hospitalization once lifetime reserve days are used up.

But beyond these minimum standards, Medigap plans can vary in significant ways. Although most cover the hospital deductible and a great many cover the Part B deductible, some do not. Many do not cover prescription drugs. Some provide benefits for excess physicians' charges beyond the allowable level, extra days in a SNF, additional home-nursing services, and so on. HMO Medicare plans, on the other hand, offer broader benefits than indemnity policies. Before you seriously consider buying any type of plan, you will need to make sure that it covers the kinds of costs you are most likely to incur.

What Gaps Are Worth Filling?

Most of the gaps in Medicare coverage fall into one of three categories: out-of-pocket expenses for covered benefits (deductibles and co-insurance), physicians' fees in excess of Medicare allowable charges, and services that Medicare does not cover.

Out-of-Pocket Expenses for Covered Hospital Benefits

Make sure that any supplementary insurance you buy covers the Medicare hospital deductible and co-payments and pays for all hospital costs once your lifetime reserve days are exhausted. Owing to the repeal of the 1988 Catastrophic Coverage Act, Medicare beneficiaries are once again faced with the possibility of using up their hospital benefits entirely.

Out-of-Pocket Expenses for Skilled Nursing Facilities (SNFs)

Medicare offers only partial coverage for care in a skilled nursing facility. Supplementary insurance should cover the cost of co-payments for days twenty-one through one hundred ($74 per day in 1990) plus 100 percent of the costs after the SNF coverage is exhausted. Look for a policy that protects you from large uncovered expenses in this area.

Out-of-Pocket Costs for Uncovered Physician Fees

One of the most important functions of a supplementary insurance plan is to protect you from physicians' fees that Medicare does not cover. Remember that under Medicare, you pay 20 percent of *allowable* charges, with *no stop-loss on physician bills. You must also pay 100 percent of whatever your physicians charge in excess of allowable charges.*

Some physicians will agree in advance to accept the amount that Medicare calculates, or "assigns," as the full amount they will charge. These doctors are said to accept "Medicare assignment." If you receive care from physicians who accept assignment, Medicare will pay 80 percent of their bills, and you will pay 20 percent.

Whether or not a physician accepts assignment, Medicare reimbursements will likely be substantially lower than his or her regular fees. Medicare does reward doctors who accept assignment by reimbursing them at a somewhat higher rate than those who don't. But two-thirds of all physicians do not accept Medicare assignment for all their Medicare patients. They may willingly lower their fees if they know that a patient is in financial distress. Otherwise, they will bill for the difference between what Medicare pays them and the fee they have set for a given service. This practice is known as "balance-billing."

Some states have legislation that addresses balance-billing. Massachusetts and Rhode Island prohibit it entirely, and some other states have set limitations for patients who cannot afford to pay full fees. Call or write to your state insurance commissioner to find out if restrictions on balance-billing apply in your state, and exactly what they are. Although most physicians who do not accept Medicare assignment strongly oppose legislation that would outlaw balance-billing, the federal legislation passed in 1989 will sharply curtail this practice by 1991.

Out-of-Pocket Expenses for Excluded Services

There are some medical expenses Medicare does not cover at all. Perhaps the most significant of these, for most people, is the cost of prescription drugs. If you have chronic medical problems for which you need several prescriptions, a Medigap plan may provide financial relief. Check for this type of coverage specifically, because many Medigap plans do not cover prescriptions.

Other costs not covered by Medicare—routine physicals, care required in foreign countries, eye examinations, glasses, routine foot care, and dental care—are also often ignored by Medigap policies, although those sold by Blue Cross are more likely to cover some of these costs. Because you can project and budget for these costs, you may not need additional coverage. Some Medigap policies cover periodic eye exams, and some offer periodic physical exams.

Projecting Your Out-of-Pocket Expenses

The first question you need to ask is whether additional insurance will help with the actual expenses you have had to bear or those you expect to incur in the next year or two. To find the answer, we suggest that you estimate the kinds of medical expenses that you anticipate. You can calculate your expenses in one of two ways:

1. Add up all the medical expenses you have had to pay out of your own pocket for the past two years and divide by two to get an average cost per year.

2. Create a list of costs you expect to pay over the next year. These costs would include all deductibles, all co-insurance expenses, all physicians' fees—that you can anticipate—in excess of the Medicare allowable fees, and payments for services that are not covered that you would probably use.

Projectable Expenses

1. One hospital deductible ($592)	$ ______
2. Part B deductible ($75) plus your 20 percent share of allowable physicians' fees	$ ______
3. All physicians' fees in excess of Medicare allowable fees	$ ______
4. Prescription drugs and eyeglasses	$ ______
5. Preventive care (routine physical, screening tests, routine foot care, eye exams, etc.)	$ ______
6. Total (annual expense)	$ ______
7. Total divided by twelve (monthly expense)	$ ______

You now have an average monthly cost, which you can use to compare with premiums for Medigap indemnity plans or for HMO supplementary plans. If your average projectable expenses are significantly higher than the premiums of the plans you're considering, you know additional coverage would be worthwhile. If your projectable expenses are lower, you may wonder whether you need a supplementary plan.

In addition to providing coverage for projectable expenses, however, Medigap insurance should help ease the burden if you were to face sudden huge bills as the result of a prolonged hospital stay that exhausted your Medicare benefits. Ask yourself how much you could afford to pay in unexpected out-of-pocket expenses. If your financial security would be jeopardized by an expensive illness, you need to consider buying supplementary insurance.

You are now faced with two options. You can buy an indemnity Medigap plan or an HMO Medicare plan.

How to Choose an Indemnity Medigap Plan

Do the benefits meet your needs? If you have been diagnosed with a medical problem, you will need to look for a plan that does not exclude it as a preexisting condition (PEC). A Medigap policy is not allowed to call a condition a PEC unless you received medical advice or treatment for it within the six months before you purchased the policy.

If you cannot find a plan that covers PECs immediately, look for one that excludes coverage for ninety days or less, rather than one that may make you wait as long as six months.

Is the plan renewable? Another key ingredient of a good Medigap policy is guaranteed renewability. At best, the plan will simply say "guaranteed renewable." Next best would be the plan that is "conditionally renewable" or "class cancelable." These plans can be canceled if the company discontinues an entire class of policies; for example, all Medigap policies in your state. Under no circumstances should you purchase a plan that is renewable "at the option of the company." You are apt to face cancellation just when you need insurance—perhaps after paying premiums for a number of years during which you were healthy.

Will the plan protect you against "balance-billing"? Medicare reimburses you for 80 percent of *allowable* physician fees, and you pay 20 percent. How well do Medigap plans insure against the difference between the allowable charge and the actual fee your physician sets? In 1989 *Consumer Reports* analyzed twenty-eight Medigap policies, sold by a number of companies.[2] Fifteen offered no coverage for excess fees. The rest offered some coverage, but only one policy paid 100 percent of all excess charges. That policy, *Consumer Reports* stated, covered "all charges above allowable charges."

When a Medigap policy states that it pays 20 percent of physicians' bills, read on and read carefully. Medigap plans may pay only 20 percent of *allowable* charges. Some Medigap policies use language that suggests extensive coverage of excess physicians' fees while actually offering a far more limited benefit. Such a policy may state that it covers "all reasonable and customary charges above allowable charges." This kind of statement, however, leaves you at the mercy of the company's definition of "reasonable and customary." If you cannot find a policy that covers "all charges above allowable charges," your best bet would be one that covers "up to 100 percent above allowable charges": that would leave you vulnerable only to fees that are more than twice the maximum allowed by Medicare.

Will your premium continue to increase? Premiums for Medicare supplementary policies increase for two reasons: One, because the claims experience of the policy warrants an increase, usually every year; and two, because you get older and move to a different age band for which the premium is higher.

While some Medigap plans sponsored by Blue Cross still community rate their premiums, some commercial insurance companies address the increased cost of covering subscribers as they grow older by selling age-rated policies. That is, they raise the premium cost as you grow older, generally in five-year increments, or bands. Some states have passed laws that compel companies to continue to charge you the premium rate for the age at which you joined the plan, regardless of your present age. This is known as "entry-level pricing."

For example, if you purchase a plan at age sixty-eight, you will continue to pay the rate for subscribers in the 65–69 band, as long as you remain in the plan, regardless of your actual age. While premiums for all age bands are likely to increase each year, you will remain in the age band at which you joined, rather than advancing to the more expensively rated 70–74 band.

How does the premium compare with the benefits? Once you've satisfied yourself that you are dealing with a reliable company, that the policy it offers provides the coverage you need, that your particular medical problems will not be excluded, and that the policy is guaranteed renewable, or at least conditionally renewable, your next step is to compare the cost of the premium to the benefits the plan offers.

A careful comparison is particularly important for 1990

and 1991. Medicare coverage has gone through a series of changes that dramatically affect the premiums of supplementary policies; there have been premium increases of up to 40 percent in 1990, and those plans that did not raise their premiums will probably have large increases in 1991.

Is the insurance company financially stable? Determine whether the policy you are considering is sold by a financially stable company. *Best's Insurance Reports* (available in most libraries) evaluates the financial strength of most commercial insurance companies, rating them from A+ to C.[3] Avoid companies that are rated lower than B+ and try to find one rated A or A+. Blue Cross and Blue Shield, as nonprofit organizations, are not rated by *Best's.*

Use the following format to draw up a worksheet to help you compare Medigap policies:

COMPARISON OF BENEFITS WORKSHEET

	Policy 1	Policy 2	Policy 3	Policy 4
Premium				
PEC				
Renewable				
Hospital costs				
a (deductible)				
b (co-payments)				
c (excess days)				
SNF co-payment				
Physician costs				
a (deductible)				
b (allowable charges)				
c (excess charges)				
Drugs				
Other				

How to Use the Worksheet

1. For "Premium," record the cost, and "A" if it is age-rated or "P" if you are protected against moving up to a higher cost as you age.

2. For "PEC," enter the number of months you must wait for coverage to begin.

3. For "Renewable," write "G" if the plan is guaranteed renewable and "C" if it is conditionally renewable.

4. For "Hospital costs a," write "Y" if the $592 hospital deductible is covered. For "b," write "Y" if the $148 and $296 co-payments (see table on page 176) are covered. For "c," write "Y" if hospital days are covered in full after the Medicare hospital benefit is exhausted.

5. For "SNF," write "Y" if the daily co-payments of $74 are covered.

6. For "Physician costs a," write "Y" if the $75 deductible is covered. For "b," indicate whether your 20 percent share of "reasonable and customary" physicians' bills is covered in full, or whether a deductible must first be met. For "c," indicate to what extent, if at all, the plan covers physicians' charges in excess of those allowed by Medicare.

7. For "Drugs," indicate whether outpatient prescription drugs are covered and, if so, to what extent.

8. For "Other," indicate whether there is coverage for services not included under Medicare, such as care received while traveling in a foreign country, eye exams, glasses, routine physicals, and so on.

How to Make Your Choice

Once you have entered the features of each indemnity plan on your worksheet, you can easily cross off those that do not contain the following safeguards:

Renewability. Exclude plans that are not at least conditionally renewable, and give a strong preference to those plans that are guaranteed renewable.

PECs. If you have no medical problems, this column is irrelevant. But if you have a PEC and expect that you will need expensive care in the next six months, eliminate policies that exclude PECs for six months.

Hospital deductible. Don't purchase a policy that fails to cover hospital deductibles and co-payments. Give extra credit to plans that provide full coverage after you exhaust the Medicare hospital benefit.

M.D. allowable charges. After you eliminate plans that do not fit the above criteria, concentrate on the next category: M.D. allowable charges. Cross off any plans that do not cover the 20 percent share of allowable charges that you must pay under Medicare.

M.D. excess charges. Unless you live in one of the few states that offers legal protection against balance-billing, coverage for excess physicians' charges will be important to you.

SNF co-payment. Give extra credit to plans that cover the SNF co-payment.

Outpatient prescription drugs. Half of the plans surveyed by *Consumer Reports* offered some coverage for outpatient prescription drugs. If you expect to incur heavy expenses in this area, drug coverage will be important to you.

Other. Are there additional benefits, such as coverage while traveling in a foreign country, vision care, glasses, periodic exams, screening tests, or other types of preventive care that are important to you? Check to see if any of the plans that satisfy all your other requirements provide this coverage.

You can now go back to your list of projectable expenses to determine how much money you're likely to spend next year in each of the five categories we identified there. Calculate how much each policy would pay toward these expenses and how much you would have to pay out of your own pocket. Choose the policy that offers the best coverage for your needs at a premium you can afford.

Check to see when each plan allows new members to enroll. Some Medigap indemnity policies sign up new subscribers once a year, usually during the month of December. These plans will make an exception for new subscribers who have just turned sixty-five and will allow them to sign up during their birthday month.

Choosing an HMO to Supplement Medicare

Instead of buying an indemnity plan, you may want to consider buying an HMO Medicare plan. You may also be offered the chance to buy coverage from a Competitive Medical Plan (CMP). (This type of plan is less regulated than an HMO but is otherwise similar, and most of what we say about HMOs will apply to CMPs.) Not all HMOs offer Medicare plans, but those that do will cover all physicians' and hospital charges in full if your care is authorized by the HMO. To be eligible for either kind of plan, you must be enrolled in Medicare Part B and pay Part B premiums. The HMO, like an indemnity Medigap plan, will then charge an additional premium to cover all the Medicare deductibles and co-payments, pay for all authorized physicians' charges, and provide additional benefits.

How HMOs Work with Medicare

There are two different approaches an HMO may use in offering supplementary plans to Medicare beneficiaries.

Cost contracts. Some HMOs have a "cost contract" with the federal Health Care Financing Administration (HCFA), the agency responsible for administering Medicare. Under this type of contract, the HMO provides care to Medicare beneficiaries and then applies to HCFA for repayment of its costs. For example, a hospital, instead of sending bills to a beneficiary who had been admitted, would charge the HMO directly for the cost of the hospital deductible, plus any co-payments that are owed. (The hospital would also bill HCFA for reimbursement under Part A.) Specialists called in by the HMO doctor would bill the HMO directly for their fees, not the patient. The HMO would then apply to HCFA for reimbursement for 80 percent of the Medicare allowable charge for that bill and would itself pay any remaining part of the fee above that amount.

If you buy HMO supplementary insurance from an HMO that has a cost contract, you are not "locked in" to the HMO's system. You can use the HMO to arrange for all your care. If you do, you will not have to fill out claim forms, and the plan will pay for all the care it authorizes. Or, if you prefer, you can go outside the HMO system, and use any doctors or hospitals you like. If this is your choice, you will forgo any HMO coverage. You would then file Medicare claim forms, and you would be reimbursed subject to the usual Medicare deductibles and co-insurance formulas.

If there is no "lock-in," and you travel out of the HMO service area for long stretches of time and need routine care, Medicare will provide its usual coverage. (Urgently needed care is, of course, covered by the HMO.)

Risk contracts. An HMO may sign a "risk contract" with HCFA. Under this type of contract, the HMO takes financial responsibility for hospital and physicians' bills. Instead of applying for reimbursement from HCFA on a cost basis, the HMO receives a monthly sum per enrollee that varies by region and by age and sex of the members. (To arrive at a number, HCFA calculates what it would have spent on an enrollee in that region, of that age and sex, in a non-HMO situation and then pays the HMO 95 percent of that amount.)

Because HCFA pays the HMO in advance under a risk contract, Medicare beneficiaries are "locked in" and must have all their care delivered or arranged for by the HMO. If they choose to go outside the HMO system—except for critical emergencies or urgent care received when they are traveling away from the HMO's service area—they will have no Medicare coverage at all.

Low-Option and High-Option Plans

HMOs may offer two levels of coverage: a low-option plan that protects you against balance-billing and covers Medicare deductibles and co-insurance, and a high-option plan that covers care that Medicare and most Medigap policies do not. High-option plans usually cover preventive services, vision care, and immunizations, and they may also offer dental benefits and coverage for outpatient prescription drugs. The monthly premium for the high-option plan may run $10 to $20 more than the low-option plan, but for most people the additional benefits are worth the extra cost.

HMOs that offer Medicare plans may accept new enrollees only during an annual open enrollment period. Some plans with this limitation will accept new members at other times if they can pass a stringent health screening.

Preexisting Conditions (PECs)

HMOs vary in the way they cover PECs. Your goal is, if possible, to choose a plan that will cover all your medical needs from the day your enrollment is effective. (It usually takes about two months after you sign up with an HMO for your coverage to go into effect; during this period you continue to be covered by Medicare.)

Advantages of Joining an HMO

HMO Medicare plans have received favorable attention from the American Association of Retired Persons in their publication *More Health for Your Dollar: An Older Person's Guide to HMOs,* which points out that "with rare exceptions, studies of the care provided by HMOs find the quality equal to or in excess of community standards."[4] The guide offers the following summary of HMO advantages:

- a budget for your health care expenditures
- preventive health care
- no Medicare assignment problems
- no Medicare claim forms
- improved coordination of services

- less time in the hospital
- extra benefits or reduced premiums
- a program to assure quality

For many Medicare beneficiaries, these advantages may offer peace of mind and additional financial security for the following reasons.

You can budget your medical expenditures. If you live on a fixed income, you know why this is important. The average older person is likely to need medical care, and knowing that you are financially protected from unforeseen medical costs can be reassuring.

You will have coverage for preventive health care. Knowing that your care is covered may encourage you to nip medical problems in the bud. Many HMOs that offer Medicare coverage have developed special programs for older people to help them identify and avoid or reduce potential health risks.

You will not have to pay excess physicians' charges. There is no question of physician services being covered in an HMO. The only expense you incur is a small co-payment per visit ($2 to $5).

You will not have to fill out Medicare claim forms. If you choose to get your care from an HMO, there is no need to fill out forms.

You will have improved coordination of services. Older people are much more apt to have the kinds of multiple medical problems that require visits to several specialists. In an HMO, your primary care physician will stay involved with your care, will review your case with any specialists he or she refers you to, and will discuss with you any questions you may have about your medical problems. Any doctor who treats you will be provided with all pertinent information about your past health problems, current treatments, and medications.

You will have someone to arrange your medical care. HMO staff members will set up appointments for laboratory and X-ray services. They will also arrange for hospital admissions and home care services.

You will not have to pay for reassurance. Patients are often reluctant to pay to see their physicians simply for information and reassurance. In an HMO, there is no financial barrier to seeing your doctor for any reason. The most you will be liable for is a small co-payment.

You are likely to spend less time in the hospital. Medicare beneficiaries are, on average, three times as likely to enter a hospital as people under the age of sixty-five, and they usually have longer stays. HMO physicians are able to call on the resources of their plan to decrease patients' time in the hospital by providing more extensive outpatient and home health services.

You may have extra benefits. Medicare offers good coverage if you require surgery or hospital care for an illness, but it does not offer coverage for the kinds of ordinary expenses that older people encounter—for eye care, routine foot care, periodic routine examinations, and medications. HMOs are much more apt to cover the first three areas than indemnity Medigap plans. Although prescription drugs may or may not be covered by either kind of plan, some HMOs with their own pharmacies may be willing to fill your prescriptions at their cost if their Medicare plans do not offer a drug benefit.

You are part of a system that is monitored for quality. The more medical care you need, the more important it is that it be quality care. All HMOs that contract with Medicare must have formal quality assessment programs.

You will be covered for emergency care in a foreign country. Medicare offers coverage only for care that is received in the United States; HMOs cover you for emergency care anywhere in the world. If you frequently travel out of the country, this provision might be particularly helpful.

Disadvantages of Joining an HMO

Your access to non-HMO providers will be limited. A fundamental principle of HMO membership is that you will receive all your care from the plan's physicians and designated specialists. If you join an IPA model HMO, your regular doctor may be affiliated in some way, but if that doctor is a specialist, you may not be able to consult him or her without first receiving authorization from a primary care doctor. If you join a group practice HMO, you will be required to pick a primary care physician from its list of doctors. This can be a drawback if you've enjoyed a long-standing relationship with one or more physicians.

You may find that HMO locations are inconvenient. If you are dependent on public transportation, check the location of the HMO health care center you would be using to make sure that it is accessible by bus or train. Find out whether you would need to use more than one center, since some plans send all patients to a central facility for specialty or after-hours urgent care.

You will have limited coverage when you travel. Coverage while you travel may become a particular concern after retirement. For those who spend significant amounts of time traveling or vacationing out of town, signing up with an HMO may create difficulties. If you live in Minneapolis and spend your winters in Arizona or Florida, for example, you can expect your HMO to cover the cost of caring for any problems that require immediate attention when you are out of town. But if you have a problem that the HMO's medical department determines can wait a week or two, an HMO with a lock-in provision may ask you to return to its service area for treatment and may refuse to pay for visits to out-of-town doctors. This would leave you with the unpleasant choice of paying all the costs yourself or interrupting your vacation to return home for treatment.

If you travel extensively but believe that an HMO would still offer great advantages, you have two options:

1. You can look for an HMO that offers a Medicare plan with no lock-in.

2. You can look for a national HMO plan with a subsidiary in the area where you vacation and find out whether you could use it for non-urgent care.

Your access to doctors with geriatric experience is more limited. Because you cannot choose any doctor you wish, you may have more difficulty finding a doctor who is experienced in dealing with the special needs of older patients.

If these disadvantages raise any red flags, you should discuss your concerns with the HMO marketing representative and consider carefully whether any of the problems noted apply to the HMO you are thinking of joining. In evaluating an HMO's expertise in caring for older people, you can ask the marketing representative four questions:

1. How many of the plan's physicians have extra training in, or at least particular interest in, geriatric medicine?
2. Does the HMO employ other health care professionals with such expertise: geriatric nurse practitioners, for example?
3. Does the HMO offer special programs or services for older people (e.g., a routine foot care clinic, medication labels printed in large type, health assessment programs, classes and printed information dealing with the problems of older people)?
4. Are older people invited to give input to those who are running the plan? Is there a senior citizens' advisory committee? Is there someone on the board who represents the interests of older people?

Commitment to the HMO

Under no circumstances should you join an HMO with a lock-in provision unless you are prepared to receive all your care from the plan's providers (except for emergency care). In fact, we think you should join an HMO, with or without a lock-in provision, only if you are committed to using the prepaid system and its providers.

If you join an HMO and then go outside the system for care, you will be required to pay Medicare deductibles and co-insurance, the very costs you sought to protect yourself from when you joined the HMO. If a non-HMO physician decides you need surgery and admits you to the hospital, the plan is not likely to pay for the non-HMO physician's fees—and may not even cover the hospital deductible, since it did not arrange for the admission. You would then have to pay $592 for the hospital deductible plus 20 percent of the allowable physicians' charges (surgeon, anesthesiologist, radiologist) plus 100 percent of physicians' charges in excess of the Medicare allowance. Even a two-day hospital admission might end up costing you $2,000 or more. You would have been better off buying a good Medigap policy, which would have covered deductibles and co-insurance and perhaps some or all of the physicians' fees in excess of the Medicare allowances.

By mixing two systems—HMO and fee-for-service—you will also diminish your chance of receiving coordinated care. Your non-HMO doctor may not work with the same physicians and hospitals, and your medical record may not be as readily available. The result may be confusion, and you risk compromising the quality of your medical care.

Special Protection for Medicare Members of HMOs

There are a number of safeguards that may reassure Medicare beneficiaries who are considering HMO membership. They include the following:

- The HMO cannot terminate your membership because your health deteriorates or because you are expensive to treat.
- If the HMO ends its contract with Medicare—thereby dropping all Medicare beneficiaries—you must be given at least sixty days' notice in order to find other coverage.

- You can withdraw from the HMO at any time by notifying it in writing; the HMO may require you to use a special form for this purpose. If the HMO is notified prior to the tenth of the month, you will return to your usual Medicare coverage on the first of the next month; otherwise, there will be a delay until the first of the month after that.
- In 1987, the federal government developed a strict quality assessment program to survey all HMOs that sell lock-in plans. Arrangements have been made on a state-by-state basis for Professional Review Organizations (PROs) to audit the medical records kept by HMO physicians and review the plan's own quality assessment program.
- Medicare beneficiaries who are HMO members have the right to request that their plan reconsider its refusal to cover care they have received. The reconsideration review must be performed by individuals who were not involved in the original determination. If the HMO wishes to uphold its initial determination in whole or in part, it must forward the claim file to HCFA for reconsideration. HCFA's determination is final and binding on the HMO. If an enrollee disagrees with HCFA's decision and more than $100 is involved, he or she may appeal to an administrative law judge. The decision of that judge may be appealed to a federal district court if more than $1,000 is involved.

Making Your Decision

HMOs have special rules and systems (see chapter 7), and we urge you to familiarize yourself with the way they work. If an HMO plan appeals to you, your next step is to see if it represents a good financial deal. Take out the worksheet you developed for Medigap indemnity plans, and add to it all HMOs that are selling Medicare plans in your community. If you join an HMO, you will not have to pay for hospital deductibles and hospital co-payments, and you will continue to have hospital coverage even after the Medicare hospital benefit is exhausted. The HMO will be responsible for SNF co-payments, the M.D. deductible, 20 percent of M.D. allowable charges, and 100 percent of M.D. excess charges, provided you use HMO-designated physicians. Indicate these facts by putting a "Y" for covered in the appropriate columns. You can then estimate the value of each HMO plan and compare it with the indemnity plan you identified as the best value.

If you decide that an HMO is right for you, we recommend buying its high-option plan if one is offered and if you can afford it. Even with the extra cost, you may be surprised at how affordable HMO premiums are for the extensive coverage they buy. (In some areas of the country, such as Miami and parts of southern California, HCFA's costs for Medicare patients is unusually high. In those regions, some HMOs with risk contracts are paid so well by HCFA that they do not charge beneficiaries a premium to join their Medicare plans.) High-option monthly premiums tend to fall in the $40 to $70 range.

Special Issues for Medicare Beneficiaries

Buying More Than One Medicare Supplement

Unscrupulous salespeople may attempt to prey on your concerns about adequate coverage in order to convince you to buy a second Medigap policy. We recommend that you find the Medigap policy that best suits your needs, buy it, and stick with it. A second policy would, for the most part, duplicate coverage you already have and burden you with an extra premium.

"Dread-Disease" Policies

Be wary of buying the kinds of plans you see advertised on television—often enthusiastically touted by a celebrity. They may offer very limited benefits; for example, they may pay a small sum of money for each day you are in the hospital. Some of these plans, known as "dread-disease policies," play on people's fears with promises to pay "double for cancer!" And remember, if the ads emphasize that you cannot be turned down, the coverage will be very limited or the premium will be very steep. Unless you have a condition that makes it difficult to purchase insurance, you will be better off looking elsewhere.

Affording Long-Term Care

If you need daily help with bathing, dressing, and feeding, and possibly some limited medical attention—help taking medications, for example—Medicare is not the answer. It does not provide coverage for "intermediate care facilities" or "custodial care facilities." The former offer some medical services; the latter provide help with the activities of daily living. Care in either of these two types of institutions is costly and, for many older people, prohibitive. Medicare provides home health care only when there is a defined medical need.

The "Price" of Medicaid Coverage

Medicaid—the government program that pays health care expenses for the poor—will pay for long-term care in an institution if you are impoverished. Although it will spend thousands of dollars a month to keep you in a nursing home, it will seldom pay the far more modest home care expenses that might allow you to remain self-sufficient.

Before you can qualify for Medicaid, you must first use up almost all of your own financial assets. Often this occurs after you have paid for months of care in a custodial institution, using up most of your money and selling your possessions, including your house. This humiliating process is referred to as "spending down." In addition, people on Medicaid will seldom have their choice of nursing homes. Many of the more comfortable and attractive ones cost considerably more than Medicaid's allowable charges. Although these nursing homes may permit a resident who must go on Medicaid to remain, they are seldom willing to admit a new patient on Medicaid.

One of the few features retained from the 1988 Catastrophic Coverage Act has improved the spending-down situation somewhat for couples. As of September 30, 1989, if one spouse must enter a nursing home and needs Medicaid benefits to pay the costs, the other can continue to live in the community, either at home or with friends, relatives, or children and can keep any income up to 122 percent of the federal poverty level (increasing to 150 percent by July 1, 1992)—up to $12,000 a year. States vary in their policy toward spousal impoverishment, but the new law puts a floor on what that policy can be.

To learn whether you can qualify for Medicaid coverage without forfeiting your assets, discuss your situation with a lawyer. Depending on your state of residence and financial situation, you may have a number of approaches available to you.

Long-Term Care Insurance: Is It Worth Considering?

An alternative to impoverishing yourself is to buy one of the new insurance plans that cover long-term care. But let the buyer beware! Many of them have loopholes that will leave subscribers in the lurch just when they most need their insurance.

Tips for careful shoppers Ask the following questions *before* you buy such a plan:

Does the policy cover you anytime you are admitted to a nursing home, or are there special requirements? In the past, most policies required that you be admitted to a hospital for at least three days before going to a nursing home. Still allowed in a number of states, this requirement is becoming less and less common. Many states have adopted a model law proposed by the National Association of Insurance Commissioners (NAIC) and have forbidden insurance companies to sell new policies with a three-day requirement.

Try to buy a policy that does not contain a three-day hospital stay requirement or a provision that you must spend a certain number of days in a skilled nursing facility in order for the cost of your care in an intermediate or custodial facility to be covered. If you already have a long-term policy with one or both restrictions, consider replacing it with a new one that does not impose either requirement.

If the plan you purchase does require that you spend three days in the hospital before you are eligible for coverage of nursing home expenses, the insurance company will review the records of your hospitalization to determine if the reason for your hospitalization is the same as your reason for admission to the nursing home. If the diagnosis is not the same, or if the hospitalization is not deemed necessary, you may be denied coverage for your nursing home care. Since policies requiring prior hospitalization are becoming rarer anyway, it's best to avoid them if you possibly can.

Is the plan guaranteed renewable? If it's not, you might pay premiums for years, only to lose coverage when you finally need it.

Will the coverage increase with inflation? Sixty dollars a day may pay for most costs of a nursing home today; in 2010, when you need the coverage, it would cost $240 a day if inflation averages 7 percent a year. Many companies are now selling riders that index coverage to inflation; try to find a policy that offers this kind of protection.

Does the plan cover home care? Most plans do not, leaving you no choice but to enter or stay in a nursing home if you need help with activities such as bathing and dressing, even though you might be able to manage at home with some assistance from a home health aide. If your long-term insurance policy does not cover home care, consider purchasing a free-standing home-care policy to cover this kind of care.

How long is the waiting period before benefits begin? All plans have a waiting period of several weeks or more before you are eligible for reimbursement. The most generous—and expensive—policies usually start to cover you after you have been in a nursing home for twenty days. Your premium should be considerably lower if you purchase a plan that starts coverage after sixty or even one hundred days. If you can afford to pay $60 to $100 a day for several months, it is usually wise to choose a plan with a longer waiting period and a lower premium.

How many years of care does the plan cover? Some cover only two years of care, even though the average stay in a nursing home is four years.

Does the plan exclude certain problems like chronic mental disorders and Alzheimer's disease? Many plans exclude conditions that you may assume are covered. Be sure to read the policy for exact definitions of what is covered and what is not; you don't want to be arguing about such provisions when you need the coverage.

Does the insurance company have a solid reputation, and is it well established? You may pay premiums for twenty years or more before you need to use your insurance, and you want to maximize the chances that the company selling the plan will be around. Check *Best's Insurance Reports* (available in many libraries) to make sure the company has at least a B+ rating.

Does your state insurance department have information about the company and/or policy? Write or call to find out whether the insurance commissioner has received complaints about a particular long-term policy.

HMO Experiments in Long-Term Care

As an alternative to indemnity long-term care policies, the federal government has developed several demonstration projects called "Social HMOs," or SHMOs. These plans combine HMO coverage and long-term care in one policy, and their goal is to provide cost-effective care that will help the elderly remain as independent as possible. A wide range of services are covered, including health care, home care, hospital care, and help in Activities of Daily Living (ADL). (These are tasks such as bathing, dressing, using the toilet, or transferring from a bed to a wheelchair.) Despite the unfortunate acronym, social HMOs have worked well for those who have signed up.

Although these plans are popular with their subscribers, it is not yet clear whether SHMOs provide a useful model for future government or private initiatives. In their first few years, the four demonstration plans experienced "adverse selection"; that is, a high percentage of the people who signed up did so because they knew they might soon need many of the services. However, as of early 1990, three of the plans had been operating at break-even for over a year, and HCFA is now considering extending the experiment to HMOs with Medicare risk contracts.[5]

Should You Buy a Long-Term Care Policy for Yourself?

The key issue in deciding whether to purchase a long-term care policy is your present financial position. Nursing home care currently costs about $2,500 a month. If you can afford to pay that for some number of years, you don't need insurance protection. Yearly premiums can be quite expensive; people age seventy-five or over might spend $2,000 a year or more. If you are well off, you would do better to invest the money you would spend on a premium.

If you have modest financial resources, what should you do? First, if you have a spouse, find out whether your state's Medicaid rules require you to sell your house before you would be covered for nursing home care. Find out also what other assets you would be required to liquidate. Next, consider how one spouse would manage financially if the other entered a nursing home. If you own a house and have a good sum in savings, you may feel it is worthwhile to protect yourself with long-term care insurance. If you cannot afford to pay the large premium these plans charge, you are better off using the money you have for your own pleasure now, and resigning yourself to applying for Medicaid should you need it.

Although the United States is probably a long way from developing a national program to fund the cost of long-term care, you may be a long way from needing it. Before you plunk down your $500 to $3,000 a year (depending on your age and the insurance plan you're about to buy), consider the possibility that you may not ever need the insurance, or that you may not need it for twenty years, and that by then the costs may be borne by a federal program. Your decision to buy is yet another throw of the insurance dice: they bet you won't need it; you bet you will.

Should You Buy an Insurance Policy for Your Parents?

For most people, it is prudent planning to have either an indemnity Medigap plan or an HMO Medicare plan. If your parents cannot afford such a policy, and if you would have to pay for their future medical expenses yourself, buying such a policy for them may be in your own financial interest.

Long-term care insurance is worth thinking about, too. If your parents cannot afford a policy, but you know that you would not want them to "spend down" and end their lives on Medicaid, you might consider paying their premiums. Before you make that decision, you should take the time to consider whether there is a reasonable chance you would have your parents eventually live with you rather than in a nursing home. If you feel you are likely to have the financial and emotional resources to take care of an infirm elderly parent indefinitely, there would be no point in purchasing such a policy.

7

How to Get the Most from the Coverage You Choose

Recent statistics show that the average American family spends $1,300 a year in unreimbursed medical expenses.[1] A good portion of those dollars might be covered by health insurance if that family were to make a careful choice of insurance plans and learn how to use its coverage to the limit.

Protecting Your Dependents

No matter what type of health plan you choose, you must provide up-to-date information about dependents. If you change your life situation and add a spouse, a newborn, an adopted child, a stepchild, or other dependent to your family, make sure you notify your benefits department if you are employed or your insurance company if you buy your own insurance. Children are covered up to their nineteenth birthday, at a minimum. Although plans vary, those who are full-time students are likely to be covered until they are twenty-three or twenty-five. Coverage continues indefinitely under most plans for children who are severely disabled and live at home; in rare cases, contracts allow coverage for your parents if they live in your home and are dependent on you.

When you add a new dependent to your family, you will

have to notify your employer or insurer within a certain period of time. If you are going to work for a new employer, find out when your medical coverage begins. It may begin with your first day on the job, with the first day of the new calendar month after you have started work, or perhaps not until three months after you have begun working.

If there's a waiting period before your new policy goes into effect, find out if you can pay the premium yourself so that coverage will begin immediately. If you are changing employers, you can continue your previous group coverage until the new policy goes into effect if you pay the premium. We advise you to do this until your new coverage begins.

How to Get the Most Mileage out of an Indemnity Policy

Indemnity policies specify *who* can provide services, tell you *what* services are covered or excluded, and stipulate *when* (there may be a specific time frame) and *where* certain services must be performed. Each time you need medical care, you can run through a "who-what-when-where" checklist to make sure that you are using your policy correctly. Be sure to ask questions about coverage before you receive care, especially if you need expensive treatment. If you subscribe to a group plan through your employer, ask your benefits administrator at work. If you buy your own insurance, your insurance agent may be able to provide you with the information.

Who can give you care? Indemnity insurance plans may place some restrictions on your choice of health care provider. Some plans cover care given by nonphysicians—for example, chiropractors and biofeedback specialists—whereas others do not.

Care given by mid-level practitioners (physician assistants, nurse practitioners, certified nurse-midwives) will usually be covered if they work under the supervision of a physician, but treatment by nurse practitioners in solo practice may not be covered. If you are planning to become pregnant and want to receive your obstetrical care from a nurse-midwife or deliver your baby at a "birthing center," you need to find out beforehand exactly how your health insurance will reimburse you.

Indemnity policies vary greatly in their restrictions on mental health practitioners. Most will reimburse psychiatrists (M.D.s) and clinical psychologists who hold Ph.D.s, but they may not authorize payment for treatment given by other types of psychologists. Coverage for care given by social workers also varies. Some policies will reimburse you if you see a social worker who practices under the supervision of a psychiatrist or a certified Ph.D. psychologist; other policies will reimburse visits to certified social workers (ACSWs) who work independently.

As employers implement care-managing strategies to control their costs for health care benefits, limitations on freedom of choice are beginning to show up in some indemnity plans. If you see phrases like "participating physicians" or "Exclusive Provider Organization" (EPO) in your policy, be sure that you are using a source of medical care that is authorized by your employer's plan. If you fail to do so, the care may not be covered. As an example, General Motors contracts with a handful of providers for certain very expensive procedures such as magnetic resonance imaging and lithotripsy. Employees who fail to use the EPO for one of these procedures may not be covered. Some employers have signed contracts with managed mental health care organizations and will cover mental health treatment only if it is provided by practitioners who work for those organizations.

What is covered? Before you arrange for treatment, find out what your policy covers, and let your physician know what kinds of conditions are attached to your coverage. He or she may be able to help you meet the terms of your policy.

Cosmetic surgery is usually not covered, but surgery to restore function often is. If, for example, you have a child with a congenital defect that can be repaired by surgery—and the repair will improve function—make sure that the surgeon notes this on the medical record and on insurance forms.

"Routine" or "preventive" care is often excluded if it's the sole reason you're seeing a doctor. Whenever possible, try to schedule check-ups to coincide with visits for medical problems that should be covered by your policy. Determine with your physician at the time of the visit that the care you've received will or will not be covered. (It's difficult to get an insurance form changed once it's been submitted.) Resist the impulse to ask your doctor to write down a diagnosis when there is none. Nowadays, insurance companies have begun to crack down on physicians who falsify insurance forms.

A few employers, however, have taken a different approach to preventive care and may actually penalize employees who do *not* use specified preventive services. Merrill Lynch, for example, now requires all pregnant women covered by the company indemnity plan to complete a questionnaire in order to identify those who may be at high risk for complications of delivery.

Women who do not complete the questionnaire will be reimbursed only 50 percent of expenses associated with delivery rather than the usual 80 percent. Those identified by the questionnaire as "high risk" will be offered referral to a nationwide network of board-certified perinatologists and specialized neonatal facilities.

When are you covered? Many health insurance policies identify certain kinds of medical care that will not be covered immediately upon purchase of the policy. The most common of these is care for pregnancy, for which there may be a waiting period of ten or eleven months. Certain elective surgical procedures, such as tonsillectomy, hysterectomy, or hernia repair, may also require a waiting period of perhaps six to twelve months. In addition, your policy may specify a waiting period of six to twelve months before you are eligible for coverage for any problem for which you have consulted a physician in the twelve months prior to your becoming eligible for the plan. (Some plans go so far as to exclude problems for which—according to the insurance company—you *should* have consulted a physician, even if you did not.)

Certain problems must be taken care of within a specified period of time in order to be covered as reimbursable expenses. For example, reconstructive surgery following mastectomy is commonly covered (many states now require such coverage), but some plans stipulate that you have the reconstructive procedure performed within a year of surgery.

Although some plans cover emergency care at a higher rate of reimbursement than routine problems, there may be restrictions on when you receive emergency care relative to the onset of symptoms (usually twenty-four to forty-eight hours). Taking a "wait-and-see" approach before seeking emergency care could cost you benefits under a policy with time restrictions.

Still another type of time restriction has to do with how *frequently* you will be covered for a certain category of service. Reimbursement for psychotherapy, for example, may be restricted to one visit per week. Some services, such as vision checkups or routine physicals, may be covered only once a year or once every two years. A few plans limit coverage to one visit per month for any given problem.

Working within a policy's time constraints may help you save money. Scheduling as much elective care in one calendar year as possible will minimize the potential barrier posed by a deductible, and may also help you take advantage of your policy's stop-loss. Let's say that you have a plan with 80 percent co-insurance, with a stop-loss of $3,000, and that you have had surgery during the year. Chances are that you have spent all, or almost all, of the $600 maximum out-of-pocket expense (plus the deductible) that you must pay before the plan pays 100 percent of your covered medical bills. If, later in the year, you develop another problem that needs elective surgery, you will save money by scheduling it before the year is over. Letting it go until the new policy year will mean you will once again have to pay 20 percent of the costs up to $600 (plus another deductible). (Many indemnity policies contain a feature called a "deductible carry-over" that allows you to take expenses incurred in the last months of one year and use them to satisfy the deductible in the next year.)

Timing also plays a role when it comes to hospital stays. Since most plans require you to pay a percentage of your hospital bill, you can save considerable amounts of money by shortening your stay. If you must travel some distance to get to a hospital, you might decide to stay overnight in a motel near the hospital, delaying your admission until the morning of your surgery. Some hospitals actively encourage this practice and will arrange with a nearby motel for preferred prices for patients. They may even provide free transportation to the hospital in the morning.

Time is also money when it comes to obstetric care. Many hospitals offer fixed-fee packages for a twenty-four or forty-eight-hour stay for a routine delivery, or for a three- or four-day stay for a cesarean section. You might shop for a hospital that gives you the best deal and then ask your obstetrician if you can be delivered at that hospital.

Where must you receive care? Certain procedures were once reimbursed only if you were admitted to the hospital, but times have changed. Many plans now have a long list of procedures that will *not* be covered in full unless they are done on an outpatient basis: for example, tonsillectomy, inguinal hernia repair, dilation and curettage (D & C), and surgery for varicose veins. These procedures may be covered at 50 percent, or not at all, if they are done on an inpatient basis.

All outpatient surgery facilities, however, are not necessarily equal in the eyes of insurers. A physician who has an outpatient surgery suite as part of his or her office setup will bill you for the use of the suite as well as for the procedure that is performed there. Your insurance may or may not pay the "facility" charge, as opposed to the "professional" charge. It's up to you to determine what your policy covers before agreeing to have a procedure done in a doctor's surgical suite. If your insurance will not cover the facility charges there, request that your doctor do the procedure in a surgical setting that will be covered.

Reimbursement for emergency care may depend on *where* you are treated. Some policies cover emergency care only when it is given in a hospital emergency room, not in a doctor's office.

Some plans are willing to be flexible about where medical care is covered, especially if you can show that flexibility will save them money. Blue Shield of California developed a pilot program in 1986 that was so successful it has since been expanded. This program was designed to reimburse subscribers based on fairness and good sense rather than hold them to the exact wording of the policy. For example, a leukemia patient had to travel to a hospital two hundred miles from home for the special treatment he required. He preferred to stay in a hotel and receive medical care on an outpatient basis, but his Blue Shield policy did not cover hotel rooms. But because he was able to demonstrate that a hotel stay would save money, he was reimbursed for his lodging.

How much will your policy pay? In chapter 1, we described the various elements of indemnity insurance that affect how much you will be reimbursed for your medical care: deductible, co-insurance, stop-loss, lifetime maximum, and UCR. All but one of these elements are spelled out in your policy. That unknown variable, the UCR (usual, customary, and reasonable), is the fee that your insurance company will base its reimbursement on, and it varies by physician.

If you are facing the possibility of elective surgery, we suggest you do some financial fact-finding *before* the procedure is performed.

1. Ask your physician what the fee will be. A good physician will be helpful and open in dealing with money matters. If yours is unwilling to discuss fees, we recommend that you change physicians.
2. Find out from your insurance company whether the physician's fee will be covered in full (subject, of course, to co-insurance).

3. If the company informs you that the fee exceeds its UCR guidelines, find out if your physician is willing to lower the fee. If your case has unusual characteristics that justify a higher fee, ask your physician to call the insurance company and explain the situation.

4. If your doctor will not lower the fee or discuss the matter with your insurance company, find out what other doctors charge. If you feel uncomfortable asking, you might find it reassuring to know that the American Medical Association, in a pamphlet it has published on health care costs, states that "you should be able to find out the approximate charge for a standard medical treatment by phoning a doctor's office."[2] Call the offices of several other physicians in your community and ask their office managers what the fee would be for your procedure. Make sure you are calling doctors in the same specialty when you compare costs. Your insurance company may follow guidelines that specify different fees for different specialties, even though the procedure is the same.

5. If other physicians charge a considerably lower fee for the procedure you need, tell your own doctor. He or she may be willing to match their price, especially if you have limited financial resources. Or, choose a doctor with a lower fee who is equally qualified to do your procedure.

6. If, however, you learn that other physicians in your community charge what your doctor charges, share this information with your insurance company and challenge its UCR fee.

7. If the policy reimburses you according to a *fee schedule,* rather than following UCR guidelines, you must deal with your company benefits department. Your company may have saved money by buying the plan, without realizing that the fees are unrealistic. If you have facts and numbers to show how unfair the fee schedule is, you may persuade your employer to act on your behalf.

How much you get out of your policy may depend on how careful you are about reading the fine print, not just in your policy but on your medical bills. Careful reading of a hospital bill, for instance, may offer some surprises. You may find that you are being charged for services you never received. Some companies reward employees who find an error in their hospital bills with a percentage of what the company saves.

Paperwork That Pays Off

How well your policy works for you may depend on how well you work with it. We recommend that you take the following steps:

1. Whenever you receive care, find out whether your insurance company will be billed directly or whether you must be responsible for filing a claim.
2. Fill out claim forms completely and mail them in promptly. If you are submitting a claim for the costs of a prescription drug, be sure to submit a receipt that has the following information: your name and the name of your physician, the name and address of the pharmacy, the date the prescription was filled, and the cost. Some insurance companies also require the name of the drug and the strength.
3. Keep a separate notebook for your medical expenses. Keep a running tally of all the medical bills you pay so that you know when you've satisfied your deductible and when you've reached your stop-loss. The notebook may also be useful as documentation if you have a dispute with your insurance company. Note the date of each appointment, the physician's name, the reason you sought treatment, the physician's recommendations, any tests or procedures that were ordered, and the amount you paid or were billed.
4. Record the date you submit each claim in your notebook, and check with your benefits department or call the insurance company if the claim is not paid within a month.
5. Keep copies of everything—bills, receipts, and claim forms. If the insurance company makes a mistake, you will need to document your position.

"Base Plus Major Medical" Plan

If your policy contains two parts, a base plan for hospitalization and a major medical plan for physicians' fees and other expenses, you will need to learn how the two components of your plan work and what types of bills each one pays. In general, base plans cover the costs of hospitalization, physicians' bills generated in the hospital, and charges for accidents or injuries treated in the emergency room. There is often no deductible, but there may be a day limit on hospital coverage; for example, the plan may state that it covers twenty-one days in the hospital.

The major medical plan usually covers other types of medical expenses (physicians' fees for outpatient care, laboratory fees, hospital costs after twenty-one days, and so on) according to the familiar indemnity formula: deductible, coinsurance, and stop-loss.

You may need to be persistent in order to be reimbursed. Some of these two-part plans require you to submit all of your claims to your base plan first, whether or not the base plan covers them. If you file a claim for an expense covered by your major medical plan, it will be denied by the base plan and returned to you, and you must then *resubmit* the claim to your major medical plan, together with a statement from the base plan showing that it was denied.

A word of warning: some of these plans may split coverage of hospital fees and hospital-based physicians' fees between the base plan and the major medical plan, according to a defined formula. Find out whether you have additional coverage through your major medical plan before you assume that the reimbursement you get from your base plan is all that's coming to you.

How to Handle Grievances with an Indemnity Policy

What should you do if your insurance company denies what you believe to be a legitimate claim? You have several possible courses of action. Your best first step is to call the insurance company directly and ask to speak to the claims manager. (Other possibilities include talking to your company benefits manager, your union representative, or, if you have purchased insurance as an individual, your agent). Since indemnity insurance companies do not have elaborate grievance procedures, your next step, if you are still at odds, is to write directly to your state insurance commissioner. (See Appendix for the address.)

Using Indemnity Insurance to Get Good Health Care

The key advantage of indemnity insurance is freedom of choice. You are free to pick your own doctors, see any specialist for any medical problem you may encounter, and travel to a famous medical center if you do not feel your local hospital can give you adequate treatment. In order to make sure that this freedom leads to good health care you must be prepared to do some quality assurance. (Chapter 3 contains the information you need to do this. But, as a reminder, here are the basic steps you need to take.)

1. Choose a well-credentialed primary care physician (family practitioner, internist, pediatrician) for each family member.
2. Make sure that he or she is on the staff of the hospital you want to use.
3. Find out who will take care of you if your physician is unavailable and determine whether the other physicians have satisfactory medical credentials. Ask whether they will have easy access to your medical records.
4. Find out whether the physician works in tandem with a mid-level practitioner and how that practitioner is used.
5. Ask about the doctor's attitude toward telephone advice. Some physicians are reluctant to discuss medical problems over the telephone and will insist on an office visit. Some,

especially pediatricians, arrange a set time each day during which patients can call in with questions.

6. Once you have identified a well-credentialed physician, make an appointment *before* you have an urgent problem. This is your chance to decide whether you like the doctor personally and whether you would be comfortable as his or her patient.
7. Use your first visit to assess service. Doctors who are concerned with service will treat you with respect and make sure that their staff does too. You will be seen as promptly as possible when you come in for an appointment. If there is a problem, a staff member should warn you and offer to reschedule the appointment. The waiting room should be clean and pleasant, but rare Oriental rugs, signed etchings, espresso bars, and the latest copies of upscale magazines may be more indicative of fancy fees than of high-quality care.
8. When you have a medical problem, call your primary care doctor first. He or she will either treat you or refer you to the right specialist.

How to Use a PPO

To take full advantage of the savings a PPO offers, you must make your medical choices from the plan's preferred list. However, not every PPO is careful about keeping its preferred list up to date. Even physicians who work with the PPO may not be aware that a specialist, laboratory, or pharmacy—or even hospital—they are planning to refer you to may no longer be associated with the PPO.

Before you see a primary care doctor or specialist, enter a hospital, or use other medical services, check with the PPO administrative office to make sure that the providers and facilities you've chosen are on their current preferred list. If you aren't careful, you may unintentionally become responsible for a large bill.

Some PPOs use a "gatekeeper" approach. If your plan does, you will not be covered at the preferred rate if you refer yourself to a specialist rather than first consulting with your primary care doctor. Furthermore, you would then have to pay 100 percent of any portion of a fee that is higher than UCR.

How to Use an HMO Effectively

To get the most out of an HMO, you need to learn its rules and how to make them work to your advantage. Checking your member handbook or calling the plan to ask for what you need can save you time and money, and it may lead to better service.

Let's assume, for example, that you've just joined an HMO and you need a refill for medication you take for a chronic problem. If you simply show up at the pharmacy, you may be told that the prescription cannot be refilled until it is authorized by an HMO doctor. If you call the member relations department first, someone there may arrange for you to receive enough medication to tide you over until you have an appointment with one of the plan's physicians.

Immediately after you join an HMO, it's a good idea to call the member relations department and ask these three important questions:

1. How do I get care for urgent problems after hours?
2. How do I get care for urgent problems when the HMO center or IPA physician's office is open?
3. What do I do in an emergency, and how does the plan define an emergency?

Take precautions to make sure you and your family members use the HMO's services at all times. As soon as you sign up, make sure that everyone in your family who is covered by the HMO knows the name of the plan and what the rules are. Discuss your new health plan with children who are old enough to be asked questions about their health care: certainly teenagers and probably any child over eight years old. Inform the day care center director, school nurse, baby-sitter, or relatives with whom you leave your children that you are HMO members, and make sure they have the HMO telephone number to call if they need medical advice. They should understand that unless there is a true emergency they must call the plan *before* they take your child somewhere for medical care. Make sure that they understand specifically what you mean by true emergencies.

College-age children need to know that unless they receive care from the college health service, they must check with the HMO before going for any elective care. The college physician may suggest that your son's trick knee needs an MRI scan; the HMO may respond that the procedure can wait until vacation, so that it can be performed by an HMO-affiliated radiologist.

If you are a divorced parent who is legally responsible for your children's medical insurance, make sure that your former spouse understands how the HMO works, who the children's HMO physician is, and what number to call for medical advice or information on where to seek treatment after hours. If the children have long visits with a parent or relatives who live far away, find out how the HMO will cover them when they are out of town.

Getting the Most from IPA-Model HMOs

Choosing a physician. Some IPAs provide you with a list of HMO-authorized physicians and hospitals and allow you to receive care from any person or institution on their roster. Most IPAs, however, use a "case-manager," or "gatekeeper," approach; if so, you must identify a primary care physician for each person in your family. If you have joined an IPA because your doctor is affiliated with it, then all you have to do is notify the plan that he or she will be your primary care provider. If the plan informs you that your physician is not accepting new HMO patients, explain that you have been seeing this doctor for some time and have just switched from indemnity to HMO coverage.

If you are not familiar with any of the doctors on the list and need help in making a choice, call the plan and ask to speak to the "member services coordinator," "member relations representative," or "patient services coordinator." He or she should be able to provide you with information about the physicians' credentials, training, and experience, and explain how to change doctors if you are unhappy with the one you have chosen. Many plans have rules about how often patients can switch—perhaps once or twice during the year.

If you have a chronic medical problem for which you receive regular care from a specialist, you may prefer to designate this specialist as your primary care physician. If he or she is available only upon referral from a primary care physician, you may be able to persuade the HMO to let this doctor function as your primary care giver; if not, you will have to choose among the primary care doctors the plan has specified.

Self-referrals. Find out what services the IPA allows you to use without first checking with your primary care physician. Some plans specify providers with whom you can make your own arrangements. Ask about self-referrals for the following kinds of care:

- eye exams
- routine gynecological care
- pregnancy
- mental health

If you have the slightest doubt as to how to proceed, always call your primary care physician. Even if he or she gives you the wrong answer, the HMO should take responsibility for a mistake one of its physicians makes. (If it did not, you would have excellent grounds for a complaint to your state insurance commissioner.)

Getting the Most from a Group Practice HMO

Some HMOs offer orientation sessions for new members. If yours doesn't, call the plan before your first visit and ask for the name of a staff person at the health care center who can answer your questions.

Location. Group practice plans require you to identify a primary care physician as your care manager, but unless there is a particular physician you know you want to use, we suggest you decide which HMO care center you prefer before you pick a doctor. You should consider three factors: location, hours, and range of services available. Before you make your decision, ask the following three questions:

1. Can I get urgent care at the center I have chosen?
2. Can the HMO quickly transmit information from my chart if I receive care from one of the other centers?
3. Once I have chosen a center, will I be committed to getting all my care there?

Choose a center that's nearest to you at the time you're most likely to make appointments. If you must get all your care at one center, pick one that offers as many services as possible (lab, pharmacy, mental health, specialty care, and so on). Even if you have to travel a bit farther, you will save a good deal of time if you can purchase drugs and have diagnostic tests done on the spot.

Families may decide to get all their care in one center, possibly from the same family physician. While there are definite advantages in convenience and continuity to this approach, they may be counterbalanced by other considerations. For example, teenagers may want their own physicians, or a wife may wish to get her medical care from a woman, whereas her husband may feel more comfortable discussing his concerns with a man. A parent who stays home with the children might want to sign up with them for care at the center nearest home, whereas the working parent might choose the center nearest his or her workplace.

Your medical record will be kept at the center you choose. Find out whether the HMO has a computer or fax system that quickly transfers necessary information to doctors at any center. If not, people with certain kinds of chronic problems may want to choose a center that is open later than regular business hours. If, for example, you are prone to painful urinary tract infections, you will get better care at a center that has your medical records (with details of all of your previous lab work and treatments) available to the doctor who treats you. If, on the other hand, the only urgent problems you seem to encounter are sports-related injuries, having records immediately at hand is less important.

Choosing a Primary Care Physician

The key to receiving good care and service is to make yourself known. Most group practice plans recognize this fact and encourage new members to establish a relationship with a primary care physician within the first few months of joining; some have formal first-visit programs to help them do this. Whether or not your plan has such a program, we suggest you start by choosing your physician.

When you join, the plan will provide you with a list of doctors, usually including their credentials. If you want more information, the HMO will direct you to a staff member with whom you can discuss your choice.

Ask what kinds of providers offer primary care. Some HMOs use specialists in family medicine; others offer general internists for adults and pediatricians for children; some plans give women a choice between gynecologists and nurse practitioners for routine gynecological care; a few plans have specialists in adolescent medicine available for teenagers. New members who have a particular medical problem—rheumatoid arthritis, or diabetes, or chronic back pain, for example—may want to choose a doctor with a particular interest in that problem and experience in treating it.

Find out whether you can self-refer to any of the plan's providers. Even though most of your HMO medical care is arranged by your primary care physician, many plans allow members to refer themselves to certain categories of professionals. Commonly, HMO members can refer themselves to plan optometrists and mental health providers, and pregnant women can refer themselves to plan obstetricians or nurse-midwives. At this time, you can also learn how to change physicians if you are dissatisfied; most group practice models are flexible in this area.

Once you have chosen a personal physician, set up an appointment—perhaps you need a screening test or have health concerns you wish to discuss before you have an urgent problem. During this first visit, your physician will find out what your health needs are and create a medical chart. If, later on, you need an urgent appointment, telephone advice, or help in getting what you want from the HMO system, you will be a patient the doctor has seen and knows.

Making Appointments

As in any doctor's office, the first person you talk to is a receptionist. He or she follows a set of rules in allotting appointments.

Routine appointments. If you want a periodic screening test or a check-up for a medical problem that is well controlled and if you are not satisfied with how long you will have to wait to see the doctor, make it clear to the receptionist that you would like an earlier appointment. If he or she cannot accommodate you, ask to speak to an administrative manager, who should have the authority to get you an earlier appointment if your position is a reasonable one. An HMO with a responsible approach to service will make sure you receive timely care in the following kinds of situations:

• You're a teacher who plans to go away soon for the summer

- You had cancer surgery a year ago and have been told you must be monitored every three months
- You call early in May for a routine appointment, but the first one available is the first week in June, and you will be out of the country
- You are leaving in a month for a new job in a new community and want to take advantage of your HMO coverage to get prescription lenses, but you are told there will be a seven-week wait for a routine eye exam
- You wait two weeks to see your primary care physician for an unsightly rash, and he or she tells you that you need a referral to a dermatologist. When you try to make an appointment to see the dermatologist, you are told that there will be a four-week wait

Urgent appointments. Most HMOs have some type of "triage" system to set priorities for their members' requests. Usually, a receptionist will transfer calls he or she cannot handle to a nurse (sometimes referred to as an advice nurse, a triage nurse, or a consulting nurse) who is trained to sort out the medically urgent requests from those that can wait. This person will discuss your problem with you and decide whether you need an urgent appointment (within the next twenty-four hours), a non-urgent appointment (within a week or so), or advice over the telephone.

If you do not agree with the nurse's recommendation, say so, politely but clearly: "I know that you are sure I just have the flu, but I've never felt so sick in my life, and I really need to be seen right away." Your best weapon is your anxiety. Simply repeat that you are just too sick to wait more than a day.

If you are not successful in changing the nurse's mind, ask to speak to a physician, preferably your own. The physician should either succeed in reassuring you—and a physician you know and trust is often able to do this very effectively—or arrange for you to come in.

It is rarely necessary to go any further than this. If it is, there are a number of people to call: a senior nurse, a physician administrator at the center (department head, center chief, or director), the member relations department, or the medical director of the plan.

Your HMO will give you a number to call if you have an urgent problem after your center is closed. Use it if you want advice over the telephone or immediate medical attention. If your particular center is not open, the HMO may operate another one with evening and weekend hours.

What happens if the physician tells you that your problem can wait until morning and you think you need immediate attention? In this situation, you must make it clear that you believe you have a serious problem that cannot wait. If you are very concerned, even if the physician does not authorize care, go to a hospital emergency room (preferably at the HMO's affiliated hospital) and then submit the bill to the HMO with a detailed explanation of what happened.

If the urgency of your problem was confirmed by the evaluation done in the emergency room, the following arguments will help you persuade the HMO to pay the bill:

- You called first and tried to use the system properly
- You had severe enough symptoms to warrant care on an emergency basis
- The report from the ER confirmed that it was indeed a serious problem

If you did not use a designated hospital, however, the HMO may pay only a portion of your bill, even if it agrees the emergency room care was needed.

Routine care. As soon as you join the plan, schedule a visit for routine screening tests or preventive care. It's not unusual to wait a month or more for this kind of appointment, but barring any other more urgent reason for the visit, this kind of waiting period should be considered reasonable.

If you are accustomed to fee-for-service care, however, you

may have formed the habit of asking for an appointment for a routine check-up, with the intention of discussing your medical problems during the same visit. Indemnity policies favor this approach because they cover only those visits that are made for specific medical problems.

But HMOs are different, as we have explained. If you have a particular symptom or concern, schedule a visit to deal with it, and make a separate appointment for any routine care that you need. You will be seen much more quickly for medical problems than for routine screening or check-ups.

Specialty care. The largest group practice HMOs hire their own specialists. Smaller plans may hire those specialists that deal with fairly common problems—general surgeons and obstetrician/gynecologists, for example—and make arrangements with consultants in the community to do the rest of their specialty care.

Emergency and Out-of-Area Care

Take advantage of the HMO if you can. In a true emergency you are not required to call the HMO for prior authorization, but if you have time, call. The HMO doctor may be able to give you important advice and may arrange to meet you in the emergency room or call ahead to alert the emergency room staff to your arrival.

You are covered for urgent out-of-area care, but each plan has its own definition of what "urgent" means. Ask for some examples of how out-of-area claims are handled. The HMO may recommend that you call the plan if you need medical care while you are out of town, and speak to one of its physicians. That physician can authorize your care and may also help you make arrangements to see a well-qualified doctor when you are in a strange city.

When you present an out-of-area claim, the HMO will take into account how unexpected your urgent problem was. For example, a woman who is seven months pregnant, with no complications of pregnancy, will be covered if she delivers prematurely while on vacation. One who is eight and a half months pregnant, or who has been experiencing serious complications during her pregnancy, will have difficulty persuading the HMO to cover her out-of-area delivery. The exception might be urgent extenuating circumstances, such as a family emergency, that compelled her to travel (probably against the advice of her HMO doctors).

Issues Common to All Kinds of HMOs

Most HMO members have no problem getting a referral to a specialist when it is *medically* necessary. But physicians and patients do not always agree on this point. To some patients, specialty care is innately superior to primary care. If they have a skin problem, they believe that a dermatologist will give them the best treatment because he or she has devoted an entire career to problems of the skin. Physicians, however, use specialists for problems that are rare or complex, and common skin irritations or rashes that primary care physicians are trained to treat do not fit this definition.

If you want to see a specialist for reasons that seem medically trivial to your primary care physician, you will have to argue your case. If you are extremely worried, express your fears. You may convince your doctor to refer you for a consultation, with the understanding that he or she would then implement the specialist's treatment plan.

If you are dealing with a very serious medical problem such as cancer or heart disease, or if you have a child with a serious congenital defect, you may feel strongly that only a well-qualified specialist can provide the necessary care. Start by candidly explaining your feelings to your primary care physician. It is likely that you will either get a referral or learn that the problem is not as dangerous as you had thought. If, for example, your heart problem is a mild cardiac arrhythmia, you may learn that any good general internist or family physician is qualified to treat it.

Suppose, though, that you have no confidence in your doctor's treatment plan, and you believe it is imperative that you see a specialist. If your physician has been unwilling to refer you, we recommend a two-step approach:

1. Call your primary care physician and tell him or her that your problem has persisted for so long that you feel you must see a specialist.
2. If your call does not lead to a referral, call the office of the medical director, and explain that you are very concerned about your medical problem, that you have requested a referral, and that your doctor has refused to make one.

If you agree to see a specialist that contracts with the HMO and make it clear that you understand that a treatment plan recommended by the specialist may be implemented by your primary care physician, the medical director will almost always authorize the referral.

Second opinions. If you dislike or disagree with the specialist, you can ask for another referral. How easy it will be to get this second referral depends on the nature of your disagreement.

If both your primary care physician and the first specialist you consult believe that you should have a particular procedure or treatment that you think is unnecessary, you should be able to persuade the HMO to arrange for another consultation. After all, if a well-qualified specialist believes you do not need the procedure, you will be reassured and the plan will save money. On the other hand, if you think you should have a type of treatment that both your personal physician and the specialist consider ill-advised, you will have to be more persuasive.

When members and HMO physicians disagree, their disputes often involve the issue of medical appropriateness. HMO physicians tend to be on the conservative side when evaluating new or unusual treatments.

If you want a new or controversial treatment, try to support your position with informed opinion or research. Track down a copy of a medical journal article that supports your views and share it with your primary care physician and/or the medical director of the HMO. If a physician in your community is a proponent of the treatment you want, ask your HMO doctor to discuss your case with that physician. You may even decide to pay for a visit to a non-HMO consultant in order to gather data to present to your HMO doctor. (If the HMO subsequently agrees that the treatment plan you have researched is the best one, you can apply for reimbursement for the unauthorized visit to the specialist.) The more serious your medical problem, the greater the likelihood that the HMO will authorize an unusual treatment.

Referrals to non-HMO specialists. HMOs that pay community specialists on a discounted fee-for-service basis may be willing to authorize a referral to a noncontracted specialist if you are willing to pay the difference between what a contract specialist and a noncontracted specialist would charge. Some plans hire their own full-time specialists or pay physicians in the community on a monthly or an annual basis. If so, a decision to send you to a non-HMO specialist would be more expensive for the plan.

You may have an easier time getting the outside referral you want if you have an unusual problem. In that case, the HMO physicians may be less sure that they have the right answer and will agree that it is important to seek an outside expert's opinion, with the proviso that any treatment plan recommended by the outside specialist will be implemented by an HMO-affiliated physician.

Of course, you can always decide to consult any specialist you choose, if you are prepared to pay the full fee yourself. We believe that this choice should be your last resort because the specialist may recommend a treatment that HMO physicians refuse to approve if they think it is dangerous or unnecessary.

Referrals to Specialized Medical Centers

If you have a serious or unusual problem that you believe should be treated at a medical center renowned for caring for patients with that particular problem, discuss your wishes with your primary care physician or the specialist to whom you have been referred. Usually, the HMO will agree with the recommendations of its physicians.

If your doctor does not support your position, ask to meet with the medical director. Often he or she will agree that the HMO will pay at least what the plan would have paid for treatment in one of its contracted hospitals if you agree to pay the extra costs your decision entails.

Grievance Systems in HMOs

If you believe that you are not being treated fairly, you should first discuss your concerns with the people at the HMO who can most easily solve your problem. If your problem has to do with access to health care, talk with your doctor first, and then with the plan's medical director. If you have questions about your coverage, talk with the HMO benefits department. If these efforts fail, call the administrative center and find out how to initiate a grievance. (All federally qualified plans are required to have a formal grievance process.)

If no formal procedure exists, write to the chief executive officer of the plan, with a request for a response within a stated time period. If you do not receive a response or are not satisfied with the answer you get, you can write to the board of directors of the plan or complain to your state insurance commissioner.

Should you hire a lawyer? Some people resort to lawyers immediately, convinced that a legal threat will make their case more substantial. Once a lawyer is involved, however, the HMO may decide it has less flexibility in meeting your needs. One of the key principles under which any insurance company must operate is that the contract is inviolate; if it makes an exception for one person, it cannot justify refusing to make the same exception for another person.

Many disagreements, however, involve the issue of medical necessity. If possible, you should try to position your arguments in this more negotiable area. There is a much wider range of judgment allowed here, since no two medical cases are ever *exactly* alike. You are generally your own best advocate in such a case.

If you have joined an HMO through an employer, your company benefits specialist may be an effective advocate if he or she believes that you have a good case. The HMO wants to keep your company's business, even if it is going to lose yours, and it may take a second look at a decision it has made. If you joined through a union, you can ask your union representative to plead your case with the HMO.

Grievance systems are not designed to deal with problems of possible professional liability but rather with contractual issues or interpretations. An HMO member would use the same legal methods any patient would use if there were a question of malpractice.

How to Take Advantage of Special Services

Ask your physician or the member services department for a list of classes and programs available through the HMO's health education department. Most group practice plans have health educators, nurses, nutritionists, and other types of professionals on staff to help you deal with problems that range from controlling your diabetes to improving your skills as a parent to weight control. In addition, sizable group practices often help members with particular problems (endometriosis, colostomies, a child with cancer, and so on) to form or participate in self-help groups. If you have a problem that you think would be helped by such a group, ask your physician if the plan has one available; if not, ask how you can get one started.

Governance

Until recently, all federally qualified HMOs had to draw one-third of their boards from plan membership. Although this is no longer a legal requirement, most not-for-profit HMOs include a number of consumers on their boards and board committees. Some HMOs, most notably the three large "Group Healths"—Group Health Cooperative of Puget Sound; Group Health, Inc. (Twin Cities); and Group Health Association (Washington, D.C.)—have boards of directors composed entirely of plan members elected by the consumers themselves. You may be reassured by knowing that many or all of the board members receive their own care from the plan.

In addition, consumer governance gives plan members the opportunity to provide input into decisions the plan makes about benefits, premiums, services, location of facilities, and so on. If this appeals to you, call the HMO's executive offices and ask how you can become involved in governance. Most HMOs with consumers on their boards also have board committees and advisory groups that welcome new members.

How to Get the Most from Your Medicare Coverage

For those Medicare beneficiaries who do not belong to HMOs, there are two areas of special concern: uncovered physician fees and early discharge from hospitals.

Keeping a Lid on Physicians' Fees

Unless you have a Medigap plan that gives you 100 percent protection against physicians' fees in excess of Medicare's allowable fees, you may want to find a doctor who takes "assignment." Community organizations for the elderly or the county medical society may have lists of physicians who will.

(See chapter 6 for a discussion of Medicare allowable charges and assignment.) If you are having trouble paying medical bills that exceed the allowable fees and wish to continue seeing your present physician, discuss the issue with him or her.

How do doctors decide whether or not to accept assignment for a particular patient? Recently, the Washington State Medical Association (WSMA), a fairly typical group of physicians, developed the following guidelines to help their members make decisions about accepting assignment from a particular patient. You can show your physician these guidelines or use them as a basis for your fee negotiations.

> *Recommendation:* WSMA should call upon all physicians to fully consider their senior patients' income level and financial situation when deciding to take assignment on a case-by-case basis. The following are recommended indications for considering Medicare assignment:
>
> 1. When assignment has been accepted for previous care rendered
> 2. When the difference between the physician's usual charge and the Medicare payment does not warrant the cost of billing
> 3. When the patient resides in public or low-income housing facilities
> 4. When the patient's income level qualifies for use of federal food stamps
> 5. When the income from social security constitutes 50 percent or more of the patient's monthly income
> 6. When there has been a sudden, dramatic drop in the patient's family income so as to threaten available funds for food, shelter, and clothing
> 7. When the patient indicates that he or she is already having difficulty paying past charges from the practice or from other health care providers
> 8. When the physician who referred the patient has decided to accept assignment[3]

Preventing Early Discharge

Medicare beneficiaries may fear they will be discharged from the hospital before they are well enough to leave. Their concerns arise from a decision the federal government made in 1983 to change the way it paid for their hospital care. Instead of reimbursing hospitals for the particular costs generated by each Medicare patient, the government began to pay the hospitals "prospectively," based on an average expense for all patients with a given diagnosis. To come up with a "prospective payment," each hospital stay is assigned to one of 477 categories, or Diagnosis Related Groups (DRGs), each with its own established price. (There is some flexibility for geographical differences and for highly unusual cases that do not fit a particular category.) Thus, each time a Medicare patient is discharged, the hospital receives a fixed sum of money, depending on that patient's DRG—regardless of the length of time that patient stayed in the hospital.

This system was designed to force hospitals to use their resources more efficiently by putting a ceiling on government reimbursement, and to some extent it has succeeded, although it has caused financial hardships for many hospitals. For Medicare patients, however, the DRG approach has raised the worrisome question of whether the hospital would withhold care at the point it began to lose money by providing additional treatment.

The DRG system does not limit stays, only payments for them. Whereas hospital administrators may pressure doctors and may demand that doctors explain why an extra-long stay is medically necessary, only the doctor may decide to discharge a patient.

There is no such thing as a defined maximum length of stay for a given problem. A hospital takes the amount it will be paid by Medicare for a given diagnosis and uses that figure to determine, on the average, how many days patients with that diagnosis can stay in the hospital without the institution spending more on care than it receives in payment. As a given patient nears the number of days the hospital has calculated for his or her diagnosis, the hospital notifies the physician that the patient's stay may exceed the hospital's goal for discharge. *Under no circumstances can a hospital order patients to be discharged.*

Why, then, do we read about patients who are told that the *hospital* requires that they be discharged? In some cases, their physicians have been unwilling to tell the hospital that the patient was too sick to be sent home. Physicians at prestigious hospitals may not want to antagonize powerful department heads, who may be a source of referrals, or they may fear loss of admitting privileges if they do not respond to the economic needs of the hospital. Physicians at less competitive institutions may not want to oppose the hospital if they fear their qualifications would not gain them admitting privileges elsewhere. Some physicians, who agree that there is no medical reason to keep the patient in the hospital, try to avoid an unpleasant confrontation with their patient and may blame the hospital utilization committee for the decision.

If you have a well-qualified and ethical doctor, you will not be forced to place your health in jeopardy by leaving a hospital too soon. You may, however, feel insecure about leaving—if you feel secure in a hospital—and you may need home care. Before any hospital stay, we advise you to discuss with your doctor what will happen once you are discharged. You should know what kind of coverage you have for home care, so that you can make appropriate arrangements.

If you believe that you are being discharged before it is medically advisable, your first step should be to have a frank discussion with your doctor about your concerns. One possible solution may be for the physician to order home nursing care, which would then be covered by Medicare.

If you and your doctor cannot come to an agreement, ask to speak to a hospital administrator, since it is the hospital's financial well-being your doctor is placing ahead of your concerns. The hospital may not want to risk a lawsuit or adverse publicity if you have strong feelings that you are being discharged prematurely. If the doctor and the hospital both continue to disagree with you, despite your insistence that you need hospital care, you have the legal right to challenge this decision. (See Appendix for further information on such a challenge.)

Appendix

Schematic Representation of Different HMO Models

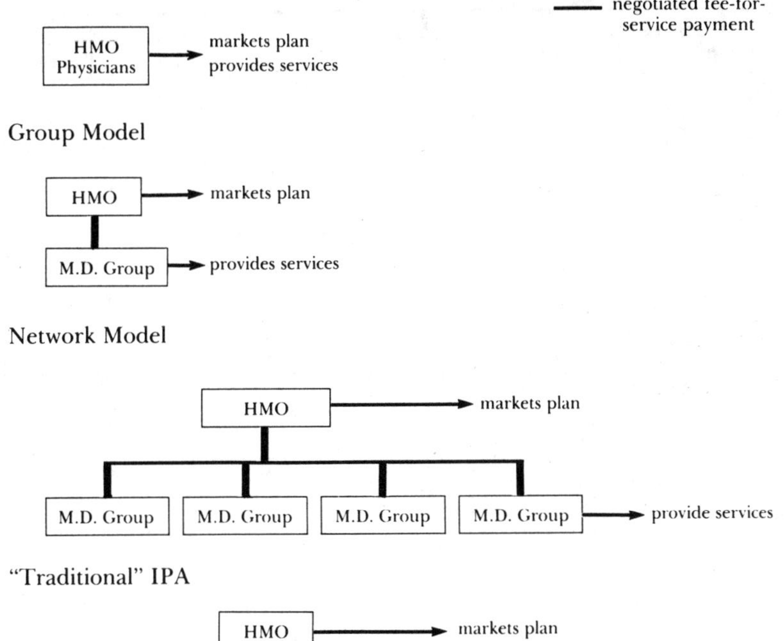

Direct Contract IPA

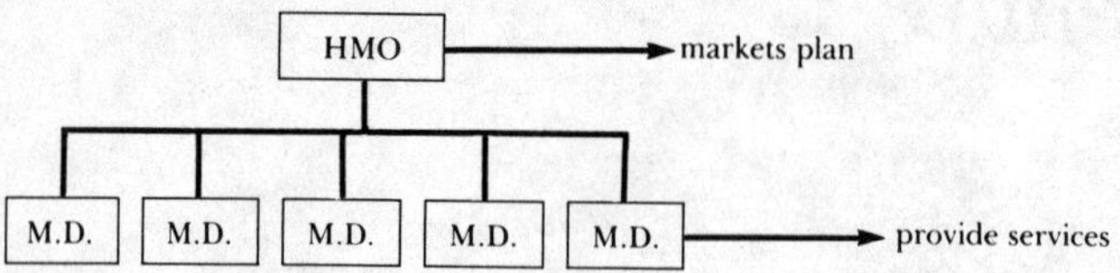

Primary Care Network

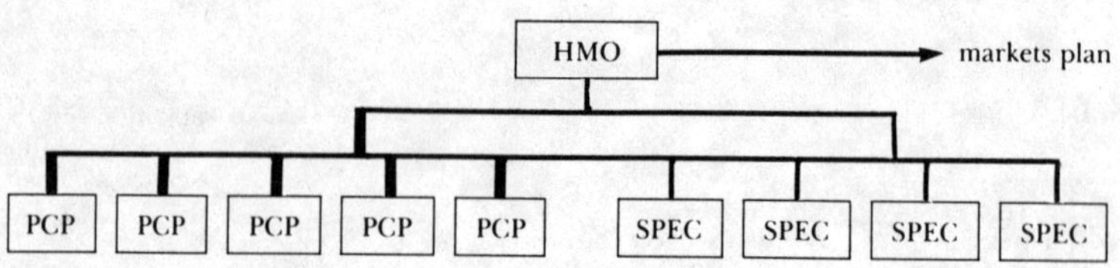

PCP = Primary Care Physician (provides primary care and refers to specialists)

SPEC = Specialist

More Information about HMOs

The National Association of Insurance Commissioners (NAIC) has drawn up a model law that individual states can use as a basis for HMO regulation. The following states have adopted it as of 1989: Alabama, Arkansas, Colorado, Georgia, Illinois, Iowa, Kansas, Louisiana, Maine, Minnesota, Mississippi, Missouri, Montana, Nebraska, New Jersey, New Mexico, North Carolina, North Dakota, Ohio, Rhode Island, South Carolina, Tennessee, Texas, Vermont, Virginia, West Virginia, and Wyoming. States that have not adopted the NAIC model have implemented regulatory legislation that they have formulated on a state-specific basis. Only Alaska and Hawaii have no regulations for HMOs. Of course, all federally qualified HMOs must operate under guidelines set nationally, which supercede state regulations.

The following two organizations maintain directories of HMOs and are good sources if you want to find out about HMOs in your area:

InterStudy
5715 Christmas Lake Road
P.O. Box 458
Excelsior, Minnesota 55331
Tel: (612) 474-1176

The National Association of Employers on Health Care Alternatives
304 Key Executive Building
104 Crandon Avenue
Key Biscayne, Florida 33149
Tel: (305) 361-2810

There are three national organizations of HMOs:

The American Managed Care and Review Association (AMCRA)
1227 25th Street N.W., Suite 610
Washington, D.C. 20037
Tel: (202) 728-0506

Group Health Association of America (GHAA)
1129 20th Street N.W., Suite 600
Washington, D.C. 20036
Tel: (202) 778-3200

The HMO Group
100 Albany Street, Suite 230
New Brunswick, New Jersey 08901
Tel: (908) 220-1388

If you want to find out if there are federally qualified HMOs in your area, you can contact:

Health Care Financing Administration (HCFA)
Office of Prepaid Health Care (OPHC)
Room 4355, HHS Bldg.
330 Independence Avenue S.W.
Washington, D.C. 20201
Tel: (202) 619-0833

For More Information on PPOs

If you want more information on PPOs in your area, or on how PPOs are regulated, you can contact:

The American Association of Preferred Provider Organizations (AAPPO)
P.O. Box 809109
Chicago, Illinois 60680

Locating Your State Insurance Commissioner

If you are unable to find the address or phone number of your state insurance commissioner, contact:

National Association of Insurance Commissioners (NAIC)
120 W. 12th Street, Suite 110
Kansas City, Missouri 64105
Tel: (816) 842-3600

More Information about Choosing Medical Services

Further Readings

For an expanded discussion of how to identify a good doctor and create a good medical relationship:

Belsky, Marvin S., M.D., and Gross, Leonard. *Beyond the Medical Mystique: How to Choose and Use Your Doctor.* New York: Arbor House, 1975.

For a wide range of information on choosing and using medical resources—doctors, hospitals, therapists, drugs, tests, surgery, and so on:

Berman, Henry S., Burhenne, Diane P., and Rose, Louisa. *The Complete Health Care Advisor: How to Get the Best and Pay the Least.* New York: St. Martin's Press, 1983.

For detailed information on hospitals and hospital routines:

Nierenberg, Judith, and Janovic, Florence. *The Hospital Experience.* New York: Bobbs-Merrill, 1978.

For a thorough discussion of how to choose and use home health care:

Nassif, Janet Zhun. *The Home Health Care Solution.* New York: Harper & Row, 1986.

For more information on the risks and benefits involved in medical decision-making:

Robin, Eugene D. *Matters of Life and Death: Risks Versus Benefits of Medical Care.* Stanford, Calif: Stanford Alumni Association, 1984.

For further reading on how to choose a psychotherapist:

Aftel, Mandy, and Lakeoff, Robin Tolmach. *When Talk Is Not Cheap, or How to Find the Right Therapist When You Don't Know Where to Begin.* New York: Warner Books, 1985; paperback edition, 1986.

Kovel, Joel. *A Complete Guide to Therapy: From Psychotherapy to Behavior Modification.* New York: Pantheon Books, 1976; paperback edition, Pantheon, 1977.

Mishara, Brian L., Ph.D., and Patterson, Robert D., M.D. *Consumers Handbook of Mental Health.* New York: Times Books, 1977; paperback edition, New American Library, 1979.

Women and Psychotherapy (prepared by the Task Force on Consumer Issues in Psychotherapy of the Association of Women in Psychology in 1981). To obtain a copy, send $5 to (check can be made payable to FOPW):

Federation of Organizations for Professional Women
2001 S. Street N.W., Suite 540
Washington, D.C. 20009

More Information on Medicare

Further Readings

Inlander, Charles B., and MacKay, Charles K. *Medicare Made Easy*. Reading, Mass.: Addison-Wesley, 1989. *Look for a 1991 edition of this book, which will cover changes in the Medicare law as of the end of 1989.*

For a detailed discussion of a specific group of Medigap policies, see "Beyond Medicare: What Insurance Do You Need?" *Consumer Reports* (June 1989), pages 375–91.

How to Extend Your Hospital Stay

Every hospital admitting office is required to give Medicare beneficiaries an information sheet called "An Important Message from Medicare." This sheet tells patients what to do if they believe that they are being discharged from the hospital sooner than is advisable and provides the address and phone number of the Peer Review Organization (PRO) that will handle their case.

Doctors Who Accept Assignment

The Medicare insurance carrier for each state is mandated by the Health Care Financing Administration, a branch of the

Department of Health and Human Services, to publish annually a guide listing the physicians and medical suppliers who accept Medicare assignment. The book (for each state) is titled *Medicare—Participating Physician/Supplier Directory.* The guide for your state is generally available in area and state Social Security offices, area and state offices of the Administration on Aging, and at most hospitals. Or you may obtain a copy free of charge by writing the Medicare carrier for your state. See your Medicare handbook for more details.

Free Help with Insurance Problems

Five states now train senior volunteers to give advice and information on Medicare: California, Idaho, New Jersey, North Carolina, and Washington. Call your state insurance commissioner to find out more about existing programs or to ask whether such a program is in the offing in your state.

Notes

Introduction

1. Glenn Kramon, "Managed Care Is the Top Plan Now," *The New York Times,* June 14, 1988, p. 28.
2. Alan Farnham, "No More Health Care on the House," *Fortune,* February 27, 1990, pp. 71–72.
3. John M. Eisenberg, "Variations in Medical Decision Making," in *Doctors' Decision Making* (Ann Arbor, Mich.: Health Administration Press Perspectives, 1986), pp. 5–27.

Chapter 1

1. "AAPPO Finalizes First National Criteria for PPO Accreditation," *Contract Health Care* (August 1988), p. 5.
2. *Best's Insurance Reports* (Life-Health) (Oldwick, N. J.: A. M. Best, published annually).
3. William A. Schaffer, M.D., F. David Rollo, M.D., Ph.D., and Carol A. Holt, R.N., "Falsification of Clinical Credentials by Physicians Applying for Ambulatory-Staff Privileges," *The New England Journal of Medicine*, vol. 318 (1988), pp. 356–58.

Chapter 2

1. *The InterStudy Edge*, vol. 2 (Excelsior, Minn: InterStudy, 1990).

2. Paul Starr, *The Social Transformation of American Medicine* (New York: Basic Books, 1982), p. 4.
3. Ibid., pp. 304–6.
4. William A. MacColl, M.D., *Group Practice and Prepayment of Medical Care* (Washington, D.C.: Public Affairs Press, 1966), p. 137.
5. Ibid., p. 54.
6. Arnold S. Relman, "The Future of Medical Practice," *Health Affairs* (Summer 1983), pp. 5–19.
7. "A Report Card on HMOs, 1980–1984," prepared for the Henry J. Kaiser Family Foundation by Louis Harris and Associates.
8. D. V. Himmelstein and S. Woolhandler, "Cost without Benefit: Administrative Waste in U.S. Health Care," *The New England Journal of Medicine*, vol. 314 (1986), pp. 441–45; and Aileen Goldberg, "Huge Losses Despite Gains by Many Plans," *Managed Healthcare*, October 10, 1989, p. 25.
9. *HMO Industry Profile, Volume 1: Benefits, Premiums, and Market Structure in 1988* (Washington, D.C.: Group Health Association of America, 1989).
10. F. Cunningham and J. Williamson, "How Does the Quality of Health Care in HMOs Compare to That in Other Settings?" *Group Health Journal*, vol. 1 (1980), pp. 4–25.
11. W. G. Mannint et al., "A Controlled Trial of the Effect of a Prepaid Group Practice on Use of Services," *The New England Journal of Medicine*, vol. 310 (1984), pp. 1505–10.
12. *Payment for Physicians' Services: Strategies for Medicare* (Washington, D.C.: Federal Office of Technology Assessment, 1987).
13. "A Report Card on HMOs, 1980–1984."
14. A. R. Davies et al., "Consumers' Acceptance of Prepaid and Fee-for-Service Medical Care: Results from a Randomized Controlled Trial," *Health Services Research*, vol. 21 (1986), pp. 429–52.

Chapter 3

1. Lynn Payer, *Medicine and Culture* (New York: Henry Holt, 1988), pp. 124–25.
2. Marcia Angell, M.D., "Cost Containment and the Physician," *Journal of the American Medical Association*, vol. 245 (1985), pp. 1203–07.
3. Kerr L. White, M.D., Introduction to Payer, *Medicine and Culture*, p. 9.
4. Stuart J. Masters et al., "Skull X-Ray Examinations after Head Trauma. Recommendations by a Multidisciplinary Panel and Validation Study," *The New England Journal of Medicine*, vol. 316 (1987), pp. 84–91; and Kenneth J. Levine et al., "A Prospective Comparison of Selective and Universal Electronic Fetal Monitoring in 34,995 Pregnancies," *The New England Journal of Medicine*, vol. 315 (1986), pp. 615–24.
5. Arthur Owens, "Will Defensive Medicine Really Protect You?" *Medical Economics*, April 18, 1988, pp. 88–100.
6. Eugene D. Robin, M.D., *Matters of Life and Death* (Stanford, Calif.: Stanford Alumni Association, 1984), p. 30.
7. Howard Spiro, M.D., "Delayed Diagnosis of Disease," *Journal of the American Medical Association*, vol. 253 (1985), p. 2258.
8. Robin, *Matters of Life and Death*, pp. 59–60.
9. "Guide to Clinical Preventive Services," Report of the U.S. Preventive Services Task Force, presented to the U.S. Department of Health and Human Services, 1989.
10. Consumers Union recommends annual pap smears for all women; tests for blood in stool after age fifty for all men and women; and annual mammography for all women over age fifty.
11. Ary L. Goldberger and Mark O'Konska, "Utility of the Routine Electrocardiogram before Surgery and on General Hospital Admissions," *Annals of Internal Medicine*, vol. 105 (1986), pp. 552–57; Lloyd Rucker, Elizabeth B. Frye, and Myrlene A. Staten, "Usefulness of Screening Chest

Roentgenograms in Prospective Patients," *Journal of the American Medical Association*, vol. 250 (1983), pp. 3209–11; and Randall D. Cebol and J. Robert Beck, "Biochemical Profiles," *Annals of Internal Medicine*, vol. 106 (1987), pp. 403–13.

12. Council on Scientific Affairs, "Medical Evaluations of Healthy Persons," *Journal of the American Medical Association*, vol. 249 (1983), pp. 1626–33.
13. Albert L. Siu, M.D., et al., "Use of the Hospital in a Randomized Trial of Prepaid Care," *Journal of the American Medical Association*, vol. 259 (1988), pp. 1343–46.
14. J. E. Wennberg, K. McPherson, and P. Casper, "Will Payment Based on Diagnosis-Related Groups Contain Hospital Costs?" *New England Journal of Medicine*, vol. 311 (1984), pp. 295–300.
15. Knight Steel et al., "Iatrogenic Illness on a General Medical Service at a University Hospital," *The New England Journal of Medicine*, vol. 304 (1981), pp. 638–42.
16. Peter M. Becker et al., "Hospital-Acquired Complications in a Randomized Controlled Clinical Trial of a Geriatric Consultation Team," *Journal of the American Medical Association*, vol. 257 (1987), pp. 2313–17.
17. Daniel Williams, M.D., personal discussion with Henry Berman, 1979.
18. Gerald B. Hickson, M.D., et al., "First Step in Obtaining Child Health Care: Selecting a Physician," *Pediatrics*, vol. 81 (March 1988), pp. 333–37.
19. Joyce V. Kelly, Ph.D., and Fred J. Hellinger, Ph.D., "Physician and Hospital Factors Associated with Mortality of Surgical Patients," *Medical Care*, vol. 24, no. 9 (September 1986), pp. 785–800. Published by the National Center for Health Services Research and Health Care Technology Assessment in Rockville, Maryland.
20. Otto F. Weis et al., "Reduction of Anxiety and Postoperative Analgesic Requirements by Audiovisual Instruction," *The Lancet*, January 1/8, 1983, pp. 43–44.
21. N. Breslau and M. R. Haug, "Service Delivery Structure and Continuity of Care: A Case Study of a Pediatric Prac-

tice in Process of Reorganization," *Journal of Health and Social Behavior*, vol. 17 (1976), p. 339.
22. M. H. Becker, R. H. Drachman, and J. P. Kirscht, "A Field Experiment to Evaluate Various Outcomes of Continuity of Physician Care," *American Journal of Public Health*, vol. 64 (1974), p. 1062.
23. Merian Kirchner, "How Much Have Your Colleagues Raised Their Fees?" *Medical Economics*, October 2, 1989, pp. 74–111.
24. Gail B. Slap, "Adolescent Medicine: Attitudes and Skills of Pediatric and Medical Residents," *Pediatrics*, vol. 73 (1983), pp. 420–27.
25. *White Paper on Adolescent Health* (Chicago, Ill.: American Medical Association, 1986).
26. Norman Gevitz, "Sectarian Medicine," *Journal of the American Medical Association*, vol. 257 (1987), pp. 1636–40.
27. *Harvard Health Letter*, January 1988, pp. 1–4.
28. Dennis O'Leary, M.D., personal discussion with Louisa Rose, 1988.

Chapter 4

1. George Bernard Shaw, "Preface on Doctors," in *The Doctor's Dilemma* (New York: Penguin, 1957), p. 9.
2. Arnold Relman, M.D., "The Future of Medical Practice," *Health Affairs* (Summer 1983), p. 7.
3. Stephen E. Goldfinger, "A Matter of Influence," *The New England Journal of Medicine*, vol. 316 (1987), pp. 1408–9.
4. Uwe E. Reinhardt, "Perspectives on Physician Payment Reform," *Group Practice Journal* (March/April 1988), p. 7.
5. "Physician Drug Dispensing: An Overview of State Regulation," prepared by the U.S. Health and Human Services Office of the Inspector General, Washington, D.C.
6. Robert A. Berenson, "In a Doctor's Wallet," *The New Republic*, May 18, 1987, pp. 11–13.

Chapter 5

1. The Wyatt Company, *1986 Group Benefits Survey.*
2. *HMO Industry Profile, Volume 1: Benefits, Premiums, and Market Structure in 1988* (Washington, D.C.: Group Health Association of America, 1989).

Chapter 6

1. "Beyond Medicare," *Consumer Reports* (June 1989), p. 375.
2. *Consumer Reports* (June 1989), pp. 375–91.
3. *Best's Insurance Reports* (Life-Health) (Oldwick, N.J.: A. M. Best, published annually).
4. *More Health for Your Dollar: An Older Person's Guide to HMOs* (Washington, D.C.: American Association of Retired Persons).
5. Lisa Lopez, "Prescription for Change," *GHAA News*, vol. 31, no. 1, pp. 13–16.

Chapter 7

1. Lani Luciano, "Your Health," *Money* (April 1989), p. 173.
2. *What You Can Do about Health Care Costs* (Chicago, Ill.: American Medical Association, 1985).
3. *Washington State Medical Association Bulletin,* August 5, 1986.

Index